SELECTED POEMS

AND MEMOIRS

SELECTED POEMS

SELECTED POEMS
AND MEMOIRS

JOHN WAIN

Smaller Sky Books

First published in Great Britain by

Smaller Sky Books
10 Brook Hill
Woodstock
Oxford OX20 1XN
England

www.smallersky.com

ISBN 1 903100-01-1

Designed and produced by
The Short Run Book Company
St Stephen's House
Arthur Road
WINDSOR
Berkshire
SL4 1RY

CONTENTS

INTRODUCTION

John Wain spent most of the 1980s and early 1990s writing his sprawling trilogy about Oxford, the city and the university, *'Where the Rivers Meet.'* It was to be his last major work: the final volume of the three was published a few weeks after he died in May 1994. Originally he intended to bring the story of Peter Leonard, son of an Oseney Town publican and subsequently history don at Oxford, up as far as the late 1960s. In the event the story (or rather the books) ends ten years before that, with the death of Leonard's son in a motor-racing crash and Leonard's own thoughts on the Russian invasion of Hungary in 1956. Wain also wrote some material which post-dated these events, which never made it into the final published work. Some of these episodes were no more than rough sketches for the storyline to continue, but others were in a more finished form. The longest of these is entitled 'The End of Lamont.'

Gavin Lamont was, in the story, Leonard's contemporary at Oxford, a young undergraduate poet who went down without taking his degree and subsequently makes rare but important appearances in the 40 or so years that the full story was to span. Despite his small overall part in the books, Lamont is a significant figure. Among all the cynical, worldly and self-serving characters, he represents a pure poetic ideal, untouched by the sordid politics which are infecting Peter Leonard's world. Lamont makes his own bargain with life, finding places to dwell peacefully while completing his central poetic work, and never compromises - even during the war he serves in the Merchant Navy rather than the Armed forces so as to take part in the conflict without shedding blood.

One of his most meaningful appearances is just before the outbreak of the Second World War. Leonard, like many people in those years, assumes that European civilisation will be completely destroyed by bombing, and that Oxford will not be spared: all its medieval buildings, its libraries, its gardens, will be swept away in a hail of TNT. At the worst moment of Leonard's despair, he meets Lamont on a dark rainy night in the college garden of what is called in the novel Episcopus, (immediately recognisable as St John's), and they spend a few moments in talk. Leonard spills out his fears to his friend, and is comforted by his quiet reflections. Afterwards, Leonard wonders if he really has met the actual, physical Lamont:

After he had gone, I stood alone in the windy quadrangle for a moment. The order and beauty of the place seemed created in order to draw to themselves the presence of a man like Lamont. I even wondered whether I had met Lamont in person at all, or had merely communicated with the idea of Lamont. Had he really been there, or had I been confronted with a hallucination, a vision that embodied my idea of Lamonthood, the gentle and meditative poet whose presence was sorely needed and would be needed even more in the iron time that was coming upon us?

The whole episode has a a symbolic, dream-like air. Lamont has made an appearance at a time of great crisis, quietening Peter Leonard's mind, and it is a pattern repeated throughout the books: at the worst moment of Leonard's doubt, the poet appears, as if to show him that the artistic spirit will survive.

In the unpublished fragment, 'The End of Lamont', Peter Leonard is in Spain years later, in conflict with another character who has made significant appearances across the years (almost as Lamont's antithesis.) This is the robotic political turncoat Carshalton, whose latest manifestation is as a Stalinist, trying to rewrite the brave history of the Spanish Civil War; Leonard clashes with him in Spain and after this clash hires a car and, in frank intellectual flight, drives almost at random across the Portugese border and into a small hill village.

As it turns out, this village is the last resting place of the poet Lamont, who has died a few months before Leonard's arrival. He has lived the last 10 years of his life in simple, almost hermit-like poverty, completing the central sequence of poems that contain his life's work. Leonard is shown to his bare little room by the village priest, who passes on to him the final manuscript of Lamont's poetry. Leonard promises that he will take it back to Oxford and make it known to the wider world. The priest, as the two take their leave outside in the dusty street, says quietly that Peter Leonard's coming to his village was no accident - it was providence, since Lamont's work, conceived in isolation, will now go out into the world and become a force for good. And Leonard, in despair after his conflict with his political and intellectual demons, is given new heart by the values that Lamont stood for.

In the published books the poet Lamont is given the role of a pure poetic ideal, the poet-scholar, the wanderer without possessions, almost the holy man, and one senses in the above episode a certain longing in the description of the poet's humble life, devoted to his art. Not for one moment am I suggesting that there is any conscious projection on the writer's part. John Wain was not the poet Lamont, nor would he have wanted to be. As a man he was clubable, social, liking to be surrounded by friends and family, relishing pubs, country walks, live jazz and conversation, whether dining in one of the three Colleges where he was a Fellow or in his local bar. He was too engaged with the world, with people and life, to have withdrawn like a hermit into a single small room in a mountain village and written poetry that might never reach anyone else. But perhaps deep within him, and in his best writing, particularly in his poems, lived a similar ideal - a way of letting his most inner voice speak directly, of expressing the continuing power of the forces that shaped him.

John Wain was born in the Potteries in 1925, the son of a prosperous local dentist, Arnold Wain, who had worked himself up from a beginning in almost unbelieveable poverty and ill-health to become a respected local citizen, magistrate, lay preacher, and one step away from Lord Mayor of Stoke-on-Trent. John went to school locally and took a First in English at St John's, Oxford in 1946. After a period as Fereday Fellow of that college he took a job as Lecturer in English at Reading University, a period he touches on in one of the autobiographical pieces in this book. A couple of years after the success of his first novel(1953) he resigned from his post at the University, settled in 1963 in Wolvercote, on the edge of Oxford, and made his living as a writer for the next forty years.

As a professional writer his output was varied and prolific: novels, short stories, journalism, autobiography and *belles lettres*, criticism, travel writing, plays for radio, TV and the stage, and of course poetry, which he never stopped writing no matter what else was going on in his life. Like many writers of his generation, his stock rose and fell across the decades; he and his fellow 'Angry Young Men' (like most of those so-called, he disliked and denied the journalistic pigeon-holing) were practically household names in the mid 1950s; Penguin published all his novels in paperback for twenty-five years, and he was before the public eye in the 1970s with his election to the Oxford Professor of Poetry chair and the success of his biography of Samuel Johnson. However the graph of his fame flattens somewhat in the 1980s, though he produced some of his best work in that decade as well as reinventing himself as a travel writer, with articles on the bastide towns of Southern France, the Scottish Highlands and the Canal du Midi - this after a lifetime's travelling to places like India, Russia and South Africa and visiting lectureships such as his semester at Vincennes.

In 1984 he won the Whitbread Best Novel Award for *Young Shoulders*, which was dramatised on BBC1, and in the same year he was made a C.B.E for services to literature. But by the mid-1980s, with novels coming at the rate of one every six to eight years, and a forced change of publisher, he seemed to have fallen out of sight; this was only partly revived by his Oxford trilogy. Yet as the high tide of his recognition drained away, it seemed to leave the true artist almost more exposed. John Wain, who had dreamed of earning his living in the 1940s as a poet and literary critic, in the 1990s continued to explore the concerns on which he had based his life's work. The mature poet, once his own relaxed and stubborn idiom had emerged, produced some of his best verse later in life, as well as his best prose: such as *Dear Shadows*, a collection of essays on people he had known who had passed on, from Richard Burton and Marshall McLuhan to a German exile in the Welsh hills and his own father. His final work was the monodrama *Johnson Is Leaving*, a moving study of the last days of Dr Johnson's life, which had its first public airing in Wain's old college a few days after he died.

If there is a unifying theme to his inner landscape, and to his art, it is perhaps the gradual reemergence in later life of the feelings instilled in him when he was a child – that the things he valued were under pressure, probably fatally so, and that their natural frailty would not survive the late twentieth century. This applies in art and literature as well as, crucially and foremost, the natural world. In his 'partial autobiography' *Sprightly Running* (1962) he describes the feelings that he had as a young child watching new housing develop across the unspoilt valley below his home in Stoke-on-Trent. There is a strong sense of common cause with the wildlife doomed to be buried under the new housing, a scenario at least as topical now as then – and he felt himself, however irrationally, threatened by the same fate. He was set apart from the local youth by his comfortable upbringing and mildly persecuted at elementary school, where the seeds of a feeling of isolation were sown. This earliest sense of being part of a threatened minority persisted, an emotional identification with the doomed wildlife which resurfaced late in his life and even in his last writings: at the age of 68 he wrote the autobiographical pieces to be found at the end of this book, in which he restated that love of the old rural surroundings he knew as a child. The evocation of that farming country on the English-Welsh border is, in these pieces, deeply infused with the realization that the countryside in general which he knew in the 1930s and 1940s was gone for ever. It reminds one that the most important single literary influence on him, one that he more than once acknowedged, was that of George Orwell, who also made an emotional identification with nature and associated rural simplicity with a child's innocence.

Oxford, in the long run, reinforced Wain's world-view. As he himself said, the intellectual effect the place had on him, a naïve 17 year old from 'the most provincial of the provinces', was unhealthily strong. Oxford in wartime gave him a further sense of being part of a minority, with most of the undergraduates having disappeared into the forces, leaving the injured or unfit to make up most of the student body (Wain himself was turned down for service because of his poor eyesight). His tutor was C.S. Lewis, who was approaching the height of his fame as a Christian writer and lecturer, and Wain became one of the youngest, if an infrequent, member of Lewis and Tolkein's literary group, the Inklings, although he didn't share their championing of 'fantasy' and heroic quest literature. Lewis's (and the others') attitude to modernity was fairly antagonistic; on top of this one of John Wain's first friends at Oxford was the neurotic poet and scholar E.H.W. Meyerstein, who frankly rejected any manifestations of the modern world at all. He emerged from Oxford with a backward looking, almost Johnsonian determination to dig in and cherish the old values while the tide of modernism swept over him - an attitude in his youth that he described, at 35, as absurd:

Always ready to dramatize a situation, I grew up towards my twentieth year with the old sense of doom, of being inexorably crowded out, inch by inch, from sunlight and nourishment, growing stronger with every day that passed...At the very time when the world was opening out before me, I saw it closing in. With every reason for optimism, I became a stoical pessimist...Looking back, I am appalled at my own complicated folly.

In 1953, *Hurry on Down* was published, his first and still best-known novel. It has been described as the forerunner of a new kind of fiction: the 'angry' novels of the early Fifties, produced, of course, by 'Angry' Young Men. Appearing the year before Kingsley Amis' *Lucky Jim*, it is the picaresque story of a young man who can neither take his preordained place in the professional middle classes nor, finally, bring himself to throw in his lot with the workers whom he briefly attempts to join. Instead, after a series of comic misadventures, he finds his own place in the world, like the poet Lamont, and makes peace with his own sense of not-belonging. What is notable to someone trying to evaluate Wain's work is that *Hurry On Down*, while outwardly it did certainly express a fashionable impatience with post-war austerity, on close examination is really an exploration of the feelings that he made explicit in *Sprightly Running* – the sense of not belonging to any particular class, the struggle to find a way of life without having to squash the personality into a unhappily distorting shape. There is a wild humour in *Hurry On Down*, and a fierce longing to join in with life, not stand outside on the sidelines, but these do not fully obscure the sense of not-belonging which is only partially resolved by the boy-gets-girl ending.

Meanwhile, to the outside world, the stance which Wain took was the exact expression of the times. There were precedents for this story of an 'angry' young misfit, such as William Cooper's *Scenes From Provincial Life* or Philip Larkin's first novel *Jill*, but *Hurry On Down* was then seen as the first novelistic expression of this new movement – which later encompassed Wain, Amis, Larkin, Alan Sillitoe, John Braine; John Osborne in the theatre and A. Alvarez and Colin Wilson as its philosophical outriders. Looking back, nearly fifty years later, it seems permissible to remark the undoubted similarities between these writers. Thematically, they do have in common a re-engagement with 'society', a returning sense of personal morality, a (hardly new) tendency to show impatience with the ruling elite, political and literary, and in terms of literary form, a rejection of pre-war "experimentialism'. However, the suggestion that some of these writers colluded to produce a self-consciously new literary movement is certainly false. (It was only a coincidence that Wain, Amis and

SELECTED POEMS AND MEMOIRS

Larkin shared a college in St John's, for example, although it is true that they remained friends for years afterwards.) The whole 'angry' tag was as much a reaction to Wain and others' broadcasting of new writing on the staid mid-1950s BBC as any considered literary judgement. Ultimately the 'angry' generation passed on from the shock they initially caused, some of them moving into a famously right-wing stance, and predictably revealed themselves, as writers, to be very different from each other.

In John Wain's case the concern in his novels and short stories was often the struggle of the individual to reach an understanding with society, a theme which his succeeding novels handle with widely varying degrees of warmth and optimism. His second novel, *Living in the Present*, less successful than the first, shows a young man struggling with the problems of suicide and murder, finally finding a way forward through love. *Strike the Father Dead* follows a young jazz pianist in revolt and ultimate reconciliation with his father, a Classics professor (which strangely seems to reconcile two sides of Wain's own life, his teaching career and his love of jazz). *The Smaller Sky* (1967) is the most open exploration of this conflict between the individual and society: a scientist who quietly escapes his suburban existence to live out his life on a London station is pursued to his death by a publicity-hungry TV reporter seeking to launch his own career. It is a rather untypical book, lucid and spare, almost reminding the reader of the sort of Continental writing once called 'existentialist'. *A Winter in the Hills*, perhaps his best novel, is the story of a middle-aged Englishman's slow entry into a close-knit Welsh community, his own acceptance of his brother's death and his final 'long-delayed coming of age'. It draws on Wain's own involvement with North Wales, thanks to his second wife Eirian's Welsh connections; the hero moves from a loneliness approaching despair to a recognition of his place in the world and the finding, always important in Wain's work, of happiness through love. *The Pardoner's Tale* handles similar ideas but in a far bleaker mood; yet it, too, ends on a note, if not of optimism, then of hope. Finally there is the huge Oxford trilogy, *Where the Rivers Meet* (1984-1994), with its hero, Peter Leonard, bridging the vast social gulf that existed in Oxford in the nineteen thirties between the University and the local people of the city living just a few streets away. Although it is perhaps not John Wain's best work, overlong and unwieldy, it did well enough in the face of apathetic publishers, and is certainly a fascinating and very well-researched social document on the city and the university of pre and immediate post-war Oxford. Closely examined, the trilogy, too, has as its central character a man whose values are of the past, in this case the perceived golden age of Victorian scholarship.

The feeling that the things he valued were being overwhelmed by a materialist, consuming society, and its allied sense of living and working in the twilight of a culture, persisted, and resurfaced in this trilogy. They are in part a record of the physical environment of Oxford that Wain remembered as a young undergraduate, before the man he always referred to as 'Billy Morris' (Lord Nuffield, the founder of Morris Motors) introduced large-scale industry to the city. In Wain's view this upset the town/gown balance that had existed in Oxford for 700 years; upset it socially and economically, and in terms of the landscape. More centrally, and more importantly, the trilogy was a defence of the 'best' of Oxford (meaning Oxford University) - its humanist tradition, its intellectual tolerance: the Enlightenment virtues, which Wain had explicitly defended in his Johnson biography. Throughout, and sometimes to excess, the narrator and hero Peter Leonard defends Wain's own view of Oxford, from hostile journalists, academic careerists and other philistines. In fact Oxford and the values which it stands for in the books are menaced throughout the story, not just by internal hostility but by the actual forces of totalitarianism, Hitler's bombers, Stalinist fellow-travellers, representing forces that care nothing for tolerance, art and freedom. In this respect Oxford is made to stand for the positive side of English (Wain always drew a sharp distinction between English and British) culture, just as the physical city, with its class divisions, could be said to be a microcosm of the nation.

In public, Wain's record on speaking out against injustice was an honourable one. Always ready to identify with the 'democratic' West, he attacked the pre-perestroika Soviet Union and in particular the treatment of the Russian writer Leonid Pasternak; in 1961, after an Observer article following his trip to the USSR, he was officially made An Enemy of the Soviet People. As regards domestic politics and issues, he also spoke out against Tory cuts in higher education cuts during the 1980s, and spent much of his last few years putting the case against the fur trade on behalf of organisations like Compassion in World Farming and Respect for Animals. The fate of the natural world was something that came increasingly to top his list of concerns later in life – so much so that many a small pile of anti-vivisection and anti-fur farming leaflets was left surreptitiously in Oxford common rooms in the late 1980s.

He also cared deeply about what happened to poetry. One of my own best memories of him is of when I was helping him compile the Oxford Library of English Verse. This consisted of helping him update an earlier selection, made in about the 1920s, and adding verse written since. He suffered with failing eyesight, in part due to late onset diabetes, but also to a childhood detached retina, and he could never, since the age of about sixteen, read as much as he would have liked. In later years his eyes (or eye; he really only had the use of one, and that was then failing) would become extremely tired after an hour or so of reading close-printed text, and I was drafted in as his reader-to and researcher. Working through the old anthology, I would give him the name of an obscure Victorian poet and he would immediately suggest half a dozen of his or her poems, usually quoting some lines from memory. At other times I would begin to read a poem and he would complete it for me, not as someone taking any kind of a test, but almost instinctively, not for my benefit but for his. This was in part a tribute to his retentive memory, which he consciously developed from the time it became clear that he would never be able to read as widely as he would have liked to, but it said more, I think, about his attitude to and his love for poetry. It was a lifelong commitment to it, the practice, study, and craft of it, and the cultivation of it too. When he was Professor of Poetry, he took the post's implicit responsibility of nurturing young and developing poets very seriously, always making himself available to them, at home, in Oxford's pubs and common rooms, or simply by reading and discussing the stuff they sent to him. His book *Professing Poetry* (1977) is a collection of the lectures he gave in that post, bound together with thoughts on the young Oxford poets of the day and containing examples of their verse. It gives a picture of just how committed he was to a continuing, changing, developing art form.

He did not welcome all developments, of course. In the late 1960s and early-'70s he produced a few squawks against the then-novel concrete poetry, sound poems, protest poetry and all the rest of it that was then briefly causing a stir. His fears more or less subsided in later years in the realisation of all the serious poetic work still being done.

As I write, Seamus Heaney's translation of *Beowulf* has won a major literary prize; Wain would have approved of the continuity of English literature's first great saga being brought before a fresh audience. In this spirit I have included one of his own translations from the Anglo-Saxon, *The Seafarer*, in this book, as well as a piece from the Latin, Samuel Johnson's *'Know Thyself'*, partly for the stately suffering of its rhythms, and partly as a gesture to Wain's lifelong empathy with his fellow Staffordshire writer.

The poems in this selection were written across more than forty years, from 1949 to the early 1990s – the span of John Wain's entire published career. He recognised two basic kinds of poem, the short, compressed kind, containing a single developed idea, and the long, convoluted, variform sort, of which he produced several. Without, I hope, doing too much damage to the longer sort by taking extracts from them, I have tried to make a representative selection of both kinds. Short or long, they all deal with what makes us human, our regrets, memories and longings, and often show a concern with the dispossessed outsiders, the forgotten and marginalised people of history, and by extension with the animals, exploited and hunted to extinction.

Letters to Five Artists, addressed to friends in Paris, Oxford and North Wales, describes the atavistic hunger that he felt came to him from his father, growing up in poverty, 'thin feet on the hot bricks', and goes on to reflect on those other hungry outsiders, the wandering gypsies of Europe and the dispossessed American slaves. That particular sequence, included in this book, speaks to his friend, the jazz trumpeter Bill Coleman, who played with the gipsy guitarist Django Reinhardt in Parisian clubs; as in his novel, *Strike the Father Dead*, he evokes the music (and by implication, all art) produced from intolerable conditions, art which reconciles us to our often troubled place in the world:

> *what bruising of continent against continent,*
> *before the two homeless songs made this their home;*
> *the plucked string and the quivering mettlesome cry,*
> *the two long journeys meeting here at last.*

History is alive in the poems, more naked and crueller than in the novels: *Wildtrack*, for example, with its section about the casualties of the Russian civil war, the prostitute and the bourgeois shot down side by side on the street corner, or the psychosis and guilt of one of the aircrew that dropped the atomic bomb on Nagasaki (*A Song About Major Eatherley*):

> *His penitence will not take away our guilt,*
> *nor sort with any consoling ritual:*
> *this is penitence for its own sake, beautiful,*
> *uncomprehending, inconsolable, unforeseen.*

In other poems his concerns are more personal. *To My Young Self* is a look into his own past, wryly comparing the restraints that he had to break through as a young man with the more subtle temptations he has to resist in his settled middle age:

> *Your voice echoed among Easter Island heads:*
> *mine shouts along a valley littered with broken waxworks.*
>
> *You had to break iron bars to get out.*
> *I have to unpick silken ropes to stay out.*
>
> *Nothing could help you but the stubborness to live.*
> *Nothing can help me but the stubborness to live.*

In many of the poems, too, he combines a love for the physical world with a keen appreciation of its frailty. In *Mid-Week Period Return*, a poem for John Betjeman, and one of his most accessible pieces of verse, he characteristically explores the countryside of Middle England, his spiritual and physical home, from Oxford to Stoke-on-Trent, and views it with a fond but unsentimental eye. It ends with this quiet tribute to his home town:

> *And now I get out and stand beside the train*
> *happy to see that steeple-crowned hill again,*
>
> *the tall church in whose shadow I learnt to read*
> *the miraculous black marks that answered my deepest need.*
>
> *In the moving crowd I stand, a silent grateful man,*
> *since this place, for me, is where it all began.*

The fragments of memoirs (published here for the first time) that he provisionally entitled first *For the Timbers of my Roof* and later on *Earthtrack*, are the beginnings of an ambitious journey through his memories of seventy years of life. The mood here is rather different to the conscious questions that inform *Sprightly Running* about who he is and what shaped him. These are more the reflections of someone sending his heart back over the years, and they move easily from descriptive scenes of the countryside around the Potteries where he grew up to meditations on the writers, especially poets, that he associates with a special place or time - much as, I suppose, a piece of music will always bring back a certain memory. His recreation of the countryside where he grew up is inextricably linked to Housman's *A Shropshire Lad*, and his early married life in Reading to the poet that he was devouring at the time, Wilfred Owen. The fragments are tantalisingly short and incomplete, but they show the things he was meditating on in the last few years of his life – the countryside, the Potteries, his own younger self, and there is an endearing touch of healthy anger about what he feels has been done to the land since those days.

It is fitting that much of the autobiographical writing included here is about Stoke-on-Trent, or the smoky place of narrow terraces and bottle kilns he knew in his youth which was not, in essence, all that different to the Five Towns of Arnold Bennett. It seemed for some years that he had turned against the place in favour of Oxford, a stance that in different forms was common to many of his fellow Fifties writers and was (of course) as much about a young man rejecting his parents' values as any genuine hostility to the place itself. But in later years he was as grateful for the gifts that Stoke had given him as those of his adopted city. In the 1970s and '80s it gave him a lot of pleasure to be an on-hand 'textual adviser' for Peter Cheeseman's Shakespearean productions at the Victoria Theatres in Stoke, both Old and New, and even more pleasure for the Vic to stage, in 1975, his own play, *Harry In the Night*. In *Professing Poetry* he looked back on the ethos of this play:

> I am giving them [the people of the Potteries] *a slice of the truth as I have learnt about it by living it for fifty years, and it is the same as their truth. Harry, when his life crumbles about him, finds new strength not from some spectacular fresh beginning, some road-to-Damascus religious vision, but simply from usefulness and productive work, from the sense that he has skills and knowledge that are needed and so can respect himself. He makes his new freedom out of the sober, industrious habits of his old slavery…This is something I learnt by growing up among these people and realizing what keeps them alive in their often monotonous and drab surroundings – alive, and full of zest and humour and courage.*

Ultimately these things are what the man and the writer stood for, and stood up for: resilience, tolerance, our common humanity, the producing of art in the most trying of circumstances, and happiness in the familiar and extraordinary things of life. In *A Winter in the Hills* he celebrates, almost in passing

... the courage and resourcefulness of human beings, their endless inventiveness, their willingness to fight back against the bitter siege of the years.

William Wain
Oxford and Rhosgadfan, 1999

A Note on the Selection

The poems are in order of publication, the earliest of them, *Cameo*, being written in 1949. The excerpt from *Feng* is from the full published text of 1975 rather than the earlier version that appeared as a pamphlet. Of the two unpublished poems, *Digging for Splinters* was written in the early 1990s, while the unfinished fragment to his second wife Eirian was probably written sometime in the 1970s or early 1980s.

Acknowledgments

The publishers would like to thank Mrs Deirdre Levi, for permission to use a quote from her late husband Peter Levi; and Faber and Faber Ltd, publishers of Philip Larkin's *Letters*. Thanks are also very much due to Humphrey Carpenter, Graham Tayar, Brenda Stones and Peter Cheeseman; Hugh, Ianto and Toby Wain; Belinda Gammon and Keeley Wilby.

Unpublished, uncompleted poem

[To Eirian]

Where the ravens wheeled we have climbed together
  wind in the grasses, hither and thither.

Your Welsh eye mirrors the care of sorrow
  but your mouth never lacked a smile for tomorrow

You call the days to your arms like children
  O many to your wise heart must be beholden.

Where the quick fish dart we two have glided
  you have spread peace when the world chided.

You listen always to a tune in the distance
  the stars' drum, the music of existence.

...From *Mixed Feelings, 1951*

Cameo

Lovers like bridges arch across
dividing landscapes. Their meetings are moments
most high and innocent, their swift silences
rich. He is her city where gardens are never
frightened by storms, and stones are tranquil;
she is his tree, his lamp of joy: no more
is worth saying. Above them the sky
hangs and seems dangerous, disliking their perfection.

[1949]

From *A Word Carved On A Sill, 1956*

The Last Time

'The last time' are the hardest words to say.
The last time is the wrong time all along.
The morning when we pack and go away.

It must be true. The angel beats the gong.
The heart floods over when we thought it dry.
Sums that work out too easily are wrong.

It is not only for escape we fly.
We fly because the world is turning round
And permanence lives only in the sky.

The Red Queen's canter over shifty ground
Is the best logic, though we learn it late;
Hoping each day to balance Lost with Found.

And if, as we suspect, it is our fate
To find out that what we lost was always more,
So that the ledger never works out straight

And each day finds us poorer than before;
Still it is searching makes us seem sublime,
Hoping each night to gain the happy shore,

To say there for the last time 'the last time.'

From *Weep Before God, 1961*

Apology for Understatement

> Forgive me that I pitch your praise too low.
> Such reticence my reverence demands,
> For silence falls with laying on of hands.
>
> Forgive me that my words come thin and slow.
> This could not be a time for eloquence,
> For silence falls with healing of the sense.
>
> We only utter what we lightly know.
> And it is rather that my love knows me.
> It is that your perfection set me free.
>
> Verse is dressed up that has nowhere to go,
> You took away my glibness with my fear.
> Forgive me that I stand in silence here.
>
> It is not words could pay you what I owe.

Anecdote Of 2 a.m.

'Why was she lost?' my darling said aloud
With never a movement in her sleep. I lay
Awake and watched her breathe, remote and proud.

Her words reached out where I could never be.
She dreamed a world remote from all I was.
'Why was she lost?' She was not asking me.

I knew that there was nothing I could say.
She breathed and dreamed beyond our kisses' sphere.
My watchful night was her unconscious day.

I could not tell what dreams disturbed her heart.
She spoke, and never knew my tongue was tied.
I longed to bless her but she lay apart.

That was our last night, if I could have known.
But I remember still how in the dark
She dreamed her question and we lay alone.

Brooklyn Heights

This is the gay cliff of the nineteenth century,
Drenched in the hopeful ozone of a new day.

Erect and brown, like retired sea-captains,
The houses gaze vigorously at the ocean.

With the hospitable eyes of retired captains
They preside over the meeting of sea and river.

On Sunday mornings the citizens revisit their beginnings.
Whole families walk in the fresh air of the past.

Their children tricycle down the nineteenth century:
America comes smiling towards them like a neighbour.

While the past on three wheels unrolls beneath them,
They hammer in the blazing forge of the future.

Brooklyn Bridge flies through the air on feathers.
The children do not know the weight of its girders.

It is the citizens carry the bridge on their shoulders:
Its overhead lights crackle in their blood vessels.

But now it is Sunday morning, and a sky swept clean.
The citizens put down the bridge and stroll at ease.

They jingle the hopeful change in their pockets.
They forget the tripping dance of the profit motive.

The big ships glide in under the high statue,
The towers cluster like spear-grass on the famous island.

And the citizens dream themselves back in a sparkle of morning.
They ride with their children under a sky swept clean.

Dream on, citizens! Dream the true America, the healer,
Drawing the hot blood from throbbing Europe!

Dream the dark-eyed immigrants from the narrow cities:
Dream the iron steamers loaded with prayers and bundles:

Breathe the ozone older than the name of commerce:
Be the citizens of the true survival!

A Handshake for
Brave Culture-Uncles

As mice tread round in drums for exercise
    Or cage-birds walk up ladders to ring bells,

So you, good hominids, mime Tarzan bold,
    Swinging on nylon ropes from tree to tree.

'Big game stampede to safety when we scold!
    At every smirk a reputation dies!'

So: thump your chests, and roar. Then home to tea.
    How like a window-box this jungle smells!

Au jardin des Plantes

The gorilla lay on his back,
One hand cupped under his head,
Like a man.

Like a labouring man tired with work,
A strong man with his strength burnt away
In the toil of earning a living.

Only of course he was not tired out with work,
Merely with boredom; his terrible strength
All burnt away by prodigal idleness.

A thousand days, and then a thousand days,
Idleness licked away his beautiful strength.
He having no need to earn a living.

It was all laid on, free of charge.
We maintained him, not for doing anything,
But for being what he was.

And so that Sunday morning he lay on his back,
Like a man, like a worn-out man,
One hand cupped under his terrible hard head.

Like a man, like a man,
One of those we maintain, not for doing anything,
But for being what they are.

A thousand days, and then a thousand days,
With everything laid on, free of charge,
They cup their heads in prodigal idleness.

A Song about Major Eatherly

The book (Femard Gigon's Formula for Death *-The Atom Bombs and* After) *also describes how Major Claude R. Eatherly, pilot of the aircraft which carried the second bomb to Nagasaki, later started having nightmares. His wife is quoted as saying: 'He often jumps up in the middle of the night and screams out in an inhuman voice which makes me feel ill: 'Release it, release it".'*

Major Eatherly began to suffer brief periods of madness, says Gigon. The doctors diagnosed extreme nervous depression, and Eatherley was awarded a pension of 237 dollars a month.

This he appears to have regarded 'as a premium for murder, as a payment for what had been done to the two Japanese cities'. He never touched the money, and took to petty thievery, for which he was committed to Fort Worth prison.

Report in The Observer, *August 1958.*

I

Good news. It seems he loved them after all.
His orders were to fry their bones to ash.
He carried up the bomb and let it fall.
And then his orders were to take the cash,

A hero's pension. But he let it lie.
It was in vain to ask him for the cause.
Simply that if he touched it he would die.
He fought his own, and not his country's wars.

His orders told him he was not a man:
An instrument, fine-tempered, clear of stain,
All fears and passions closed up like a fan:
No more volition than his aeroplane.

But now he fought to win his manhood back.
Steep from the sunset of his pain he flew
Against the darkness in that last attack.
It was for love he fought, to make that true.

II

To take life is always to die a little: to stop
any feeling and moving contrivance, however ugly,

unnecessary, or hateful, is to reduce by so much the total
of life there is. And that is to die a little.

To take the life of an enemy is to help him,
a little, towards destroying your own. Indeed, that is why
we hate our enemies: because they force us to kill them.
A murderer hides the dead man in the ground:
but his crime rears up and topples on to the living,
for it is they who now must hunt the murderer,
murder him, and hide him in the ground: it is they
who now feel the touch of death cold in their bones.

Animals hate death. A trapped fox will gnaw
through his own leg: it is so important to live
that he forgives himself the agony,
consenting, for life's sake, to the desperate teeth
grating through bone and pulp, the gasping yelps.

That is the reason the trapper hates the fox.
You think the trapper doesn't hate the fox?
But he does, and the fox can tell how much.
It is not the fox's teeth that grind his bones,
It is the trapper's. It is the trapper, there,
Who keeps his head down, gnawing, hour after hour.

And the people the trapper works for, they are there too,
heads down beside the trap, gnawing away.
Why shouldn't they hate the fox? Their cheeks are smeared
with his rank blood, and on their tongues his bone
being splintered, feels uncomfortably sharp.

So once Major Eatherly hated the Japanese.

III

Hell is a furnace, so the wise men taught.
The punishment for sin is to be broiled.
A glowing coal for every sinful thought.

The heat of God's great furnace ate up sin,
Which whispered up in smoke or fell in ash:
So that each hour a new hour could begin.

So fire was holy, though it tortured souls,
The sinners' anguish never ceased, but still
Their sin was burnt from them by shining coals.

Hell fried the criminal but burnt the crime,
Purged where it punished, healed where it destroyed:
It was a stove that warmed the rooms of time.

No man begrudged the flames their appetite.
All were afraid of fire, yet none rebelled.
The wise men taught that hell was just and right.

'The soul desires its necessary dread:
Only among the thorns can patience weave
A bower where the mind can make its bed.'

Even the holy saints whose patient jaws
Chewed bitter rind and hands raised up the dead
Were chestnuts roasted at God's furnace doors.

The wise men passed. The clever men appeared.
They ruled that hell be called a pumpkin face.
They robbed the soul of what it justly feared.
Coal after coal the fires of hell went out.
Their heat no longer warmed the rooms of time,
Which glistened now with fluorescent doubt.

The chilly saints went striding up and down
To warm their blood with useful exercise.
They rolled like conkers through the draughty town.

Those emblematic flames sank down to rest,
But metaphysical fire can not go out:
Men ran from devils they had dispossessed,

And felt within their skulls the dancing heat
No longer stored in God's deep boiler-room.
Fire scorched their temples, frostbite chewed their feet.

That parasitic fire could race and climb
More swiftly than the stately flames of hell.
Its fuel gone, it licked the beams of time.

So time dried out and youngest hearts grew old
The smoky minutes cracked and broke apart.
The world was roasting but the men were cold.

Now from this pain worse pain was brought to birth,
More hate, more anguish, till at last they cried,
'Release this fire to gnaw the crusty earth:

Make it a flame that's obvious to sight
And let us say we kindled it ourselves,
To split the skulls of men and let in light.

Since death is camped among us, wish him joy,
Invite him to our table and our games.
We cannot judge, but we can still destroy.'

And so the curtains of the mind were drawn.
Men conjured hell a first, a second time:
And Major Eatherly took off at dawn.

IV

Suppose a sea-bird,
its wings stuck down with oil, riding the waves
 in no direction, under the storm-clouds, helpless,
lifted for an instant by each moving billow
to scan the meaningless horizon, helpless,
helpless, and the storms coming, and its wings dead,
its bird-nature dead:
Imagine this castaway,
loved, perhaps, by the Creator, and yet abandoned,
mocked by the flashing scales of the fish beneath it,
who leap, twist, dive, as free of the wide sea
as formerly the bird of the wide sky,
now helpless, starving, a prisoner of the surface,
unable to dive or rise: this is your emblem.
Take away the bird, let it be drowned
in the steep black waves of the storm, let it be broken
against rocks in the morning light, too faint to swim:
take away the bird, but keep the emblem.

It is the emblem of Major Eatherly,
who looked round quickly from the height of each wave,
but saw no land, only the rim of the sky
into which he was not free to rise, or the silver
gleam of the mocking scales of the fish diving
where he was not free to dive.
Men have clung always to emblems,
to tokens of absolution from their sins.
Once it was the scapegoat driven out,
bearing its load of guilt under the empty sky
until its shape was lost, merged in the scrub.

Now we are civilized, there is no wild heath.
Instead of the nimble scapegoat running out
to be lost under the wild and empty sky,
the load of guilt is packed into prison walls,
and men file inward through the heavy doors.

But now the image, too, is obsolete.
The Major entering prison is no scapegoat.
His penitence will not take away our guilt,
nor sort with any consoling ritual:
this is penitence for its own sake, beautiful,
uncomprehending, inconsolable, unforeseen.
He is not in prison for his penitence:
it is no outrage to our law that he wakes
with cries of pity on his parching lips.
We do not punish him for cries or nightmares.
We punish him for stealing things from stores.

O, give his pension to the storekeeper.
Tell him it is the price of all our souls.
But do not trouble to unlock the door
and bring the Major out into the sun.
Leave him: it is all one: perhaps his nightmares
grow cooler in the twilight of the prison.
Leave him; if he is sleeping, come away.
But lay a folded paper by his head,
nothing official or embossed, a page
tom from your notebook, and the words in pencil.
Say nothing of love, or thanks, or penitence:
say only 'Eatherly, we have your message.'

From *Wildtrack (1965)*

The Rib

Sonnet to Jeanne Duval

Honey and feathers, silk of the inside lip
thick breath, hot heart, bind trembling at the knees
her lacing fronds, his urgent slide and grip:
the sensual symphony is scored for these,

and these you gave more still: the subtle drums,
spilt coffee on a white and starchy cloth
(through pampas grass the svelte procession comes,
the cool delicious taper claims its moth).

Only those unseen wings within him flapped
wild to be soaring in unperfumed air.
They itched beneath his skin. He paced the room,

sick with that throbbing pain, but flew nowhere.
His naked shoulders never grew a plume.
It was his lust, not yours, that held him trapped.

Hold tight for a steep dive. Bolt your
stomach into place, Jack. An insanely
intrepid dive through the steep surprising
air. Then smack into (with a plume
of spray) the salt water of our beginnings.
The bitter water that gives life. The end
of all our dreams of coolness and purity.
But first, a climb. Our dive starts from the
spindly ladders of a cosmic farce.

The day God slipped Adam a Mickey Finn!

Did you ever hear tell of it?
Well, Genesis is built
 around belly-laughs but this one
is a boffo. The burlesque houses
of all time echo with that roar
of helpless laughter, Grimaldi,
Little Tich, W.C. Fields, you are
made truly after the image of God. To squirt
water from your button-hole, squelch
a custard-pie right in that sober citizen's
well-shaven jowls, that's true piety.
                              No disrespect,
I like jokes myself. They help one to face
seriousness, by coming at it sidelong.
But this was *the most!* Think of it: he's
lonely, tells the Chief he needs a girl.
It's creepy in the evenings, with no one
to answer your voice, or tell you please
to make up the stove. Eden? It's no
great draw without someone along to talk to
about how nice it is.
                              So the Chief
says, Yes, all right, and then
WHAM! slips him a knock-out drop. Imagine that!

Ay, thou poor ghost, we will imagine that.
That sleep of Adam's, that thick restless swoon,
that coma hung with shadows and sharp dreams,
snakes crawling down the walls, fat spiders in
the bath (look that one up in Freud, fellows),
eyes sealed by God's occluding touch, teeth clenched,
look how his hands open and shut – he wants
to fight the beasts that attack him in his dream!

Hear him keep moaning? Adam, I would not
wish such a sleep on you.
                                    But that's not all!
The act gets better! What a genius, this
cosmic comedian. Out of his bag
he takes a jemmy and a silken mask.
A choker round his throat, a greasy cap.
He's going in for burglary! Before our eyes
he opens up the straight man's side and takes
 – you'd never guess it – one of his ribs. Yes, you
heard me! I thought I'd never stop laughing. The
theatre was shaking, even the usherettes
couldn't stop watching the show. Why, I'd
go crazy if I had to watch the act
again. It was *too much*.
                                    He takes this rib –
now look, ask anybody, don't believe me –
and says to him (still lying there asleep)
'You asked for it,' he says, 'you poor bastard' (or
something like that) and getting out some tools
and welding equipment, right there before our eyes,
he makes it into a WOMAN!
                                    Well, you can
imagine how that brought the house down. I can
still hear the way they clapped and cheered. Well, I mean!
Conjuring on top of an act like that!
'Okay,' he says, 'it's all
over,' and the straight
man, Adam, gets up and takes a bow,
then all of a sudden he says, 'Where's my
RIB!' and down comes his hand on that side – 'Hey!
Come back here! I'm a rib short!' Laugh? They
started again, till I thought they'd die. Honest!
I'll give him that, this Adam was quite
good in the part. I mean, he made it live.

'Where's that rib?' he says again, and 'Help!'
Just as if anyone could
help him! So of course everyone laughed
again. And *then* – just picture it! – he comes
slap face to face with this babe!

Well, after that the band just had to start
playing and the stage was cleared
for the performing seals.
                    What else?
A trouper knows when an act reaches its
natural finish. No one could laugh any more. I
found
tears on my face. That's how hard I'd been
either laughing, or something.
                    Well, I mean…

Post-operational

His eyelids opened. Light hammered on his nerves.
The tall grass heaved, with fever or desire.
The garden rocked him with its gentle curves.

The loneliness that coiled its rusty wire
about his heart, had parted. He was free.
Love shimmered like the air above a fire.

This was the miracle that had to be.
Naked, confiding, near enough to touch,
motionless in the moving light stood she.

Was he not blest beyond analysis?
His body had no doubts: its good was here:
and, dolphin-jumping in those waves of bliss,

worshipped the moon that burned so hard and clear,
worshipped the tides that made the waters dance.

O gentle earth! O crystal atmosphere!
Yet there was fear within his avid glance.

To me it was highly comick, to see the grave Philosopher – the Rambler –
toying with a Highland beauty! – But what could he do? He must have been
surly, and weak too, had he not behaved as he did. He would have been
laughed at, and not more respected, though less loved.

Boswell, The Journal of a Tour to the Hebrides
with Samuel Johnson LL.D., 1786

The Highland Girl contemplates Samuel Johnson

They sat me on his knee for a joke, after dinner.
At first, I was afraid

The fire was warm, and he sweated. My body felt heavy as a pony's.

Torchlight danced on his forehead:
I wanted to touch his eyes,
They were the colour of longing.

The men raised their glasses, and laughed
Everybody talked very loud.
I would not have been afraid to comfort him,
Had they been quiet.

He held my hand a moment, then let me go. In the night, I woke,
roused by my own weeping.

Sonnet: Act IV, Scene iii

Paint till a horse may mire upon your face!'
Mad Timon screamed to those two pleasure-girls,
Raving to drown them in his own disgrace:
What did they answer? Shrug, and toss their curls?

Furs, silks, fine hangings, asses' milk, and pearls
Lying in cups of wine: a scented place
Among the cushions: spasms and cunning twirls,
The stallion member upright as a mace –

Things without words! Talk was a stink of breath.
Bodies like theirs were made to drive men mad:
What would he have them do? Scrub kitchen floors?

Years later, dying amid rags and sores,
They thought of Timon's frenzy, and were glad:
His curses warmed their blood, that cooled towards death.

From *Letters To Five Artists (1969)*

Introductory Poem

addressed to all the friends to whom these Poems are written: about Exile,
and a Roman Poet on a Ship, and a Modern poet at an airport,and Red
Indians, and Horsemen on the Ice, and a Boy in 1900

The salt wind carries no land-smells. Even
the birds have gone back. Indifferent, they
scream on the cliffs, watch for the next boat
setting out.
                Now the world is water.
Soil must have fed these timbers long ago,
when I had no name. Now those packed grains
root-sheltering, calm, warmed with Italian sun
are a memory. Their world, like mine, is the waves
the bearded rocks far under the waves, and the monsters
our minds cannot guess at, waiting there.
Even my mind?

                So fed with prodigies,
instructed in the suddenness of change,
beast's head, arms of a shrub? A girl's
smooth-running limbs turned to a sliding stream?

Even now, cast out, shamed, it is the same mind,
made nimble by leaping among prodigies:

I, if anyone, could name the unnamed who swim
mindlessly waiting in their salty gloom?
No. I fear them too much. Water changes all.

I, lover of women, those swelling gourds,
I, devotee of liquefaction: shape
dissolved in shape, stiff blood-crammed pleasure
dissolved in warmth and wetness: I, the singer
of change and melting, the lazy river
of pleasure winding through the seasons,
the girls new-named, new-faced, but always the same
girl:
I, now, to learn about water!
                    To hear the creak
of the strained ropes, the loud complaint
of timbers sawn from their green and changing trees,
planed, caulked, sent floating far from the smell of
land:
to lie on this wooden bunk, lonely and sick
and hear the merciless waves drum on the hull
telling me:
                    this, after all, is the nature of water!

The baby floats in a living pond:
                    The grown man
thirsts for the eager juice of a ripe girl.
Wetness, wetness!
                    fountains in the dusty squares,
the quick live jet that danced in the dry air,
the splash and cool drip over the stone lip,
like love, like easy love:
haunches and breasts like ripe halves of a peach!
Now water prods and slaps me purple. Deep
in its belly the empty-eyed
monsters hide.
                    Was this always
                    true? Did water breed monsters, predatory
teeth honed for a poet's flesh, from the beginning?

Ars Amatoria. That thirst undid me.
I changed. I wrote of change. Of how
life danced, and danced, and never would be still.
This, too, was thirst: was thirst for the same drink,
for heat and liquid change liquid and heat,
men alter girls, girls change the lives of men:
but still the dusty throat
cried thirst, and only thirst, chewed my dry lines
and drank the salty juice, and cried more thirst,

and after nine years the unreachable man
 with a god's mask, took from a slave's hand
 his golden stylus and wrote down my name,
 snapped shut the blazing jewel-case of Rome
with me outside, crying, for ever outside.

Liquid, liquid undid me.
                         Washed, floated
away out of memory. Soft girls
trapped my thoughts hard. These waves
can beat timber to a pulp.
To learn about water...

Publius Ovidius Naso, this is you!

You, and not only you. The poet's flesh
is always divided and swallowed among whispers.
Whisper of grain on grain, of undersea
siftings, of ritual enacted without passion,
enacted so that the channel shall stay open
to belief, to passion, to the trembling FIAT.

You, Ovidius, and not only you, are exiled.

BOAC announce the departure of their flight
whateveritis
will passengers for this flight please
go to the top of the main staircase

See him rise from his nervous seat
flight-bag and magazines clutched in his hand
stomach already soothed with Dramamine
Dogrose, the poet in a drip-dry suit,
on his way to an

INTERNATIONAL CULTURAL CONFERENCE (fare paid,
hotel arranged: now, Dogrose, you're
an established poet who gets asked to conferences.
Friend, go up higher:
Go to the top of the main staircase!)

Adriatic waves thump the hull. The big jets
scream like trapped gulls out on the tarmac.
Gales of the sea trapped permanently in metal.
Dogrose, neat-suited. Dramamined, a true
poet with his sea-water blood
pumping through valves of indolence and lust,
shy, watchful, quick to detect a slight,
haunted by rhythms of indifferent drums,
stung out of lethargy by images
which touch his flesh like loved fingers, he rises,
this poet, and obeys the metal speaker:

go to the top of the main staircase
go to the top of the main staircase

wave after wave of voyagers, outwardly
calm with discipline and information,
inwardly shrilling like electric bells

(who am I? what will become of me? WHERE
IS HOME? are they going to kill me?)

go to the top of the main staircase

the exact procedure of a slaughterhouse
The herd, horns clicking, eyes rolling in fear,

bawling and fouling the neat passageway,
go to the top of the main staircase
where their necks are automatically, neatly, broken.

So Dogrose on his way to represent
poetry, the controlling agony, the creative
agony in the formal garden, goes
with the herd, to the top of the main staircase.

Relegatio. Technically the milder of the two Roman
forms of banishment. The other, *exsilium,* involved loss
of citizenship and confiscation of property, but at least
the *exsul* was free to wander the whole earth save within
a prescribed radius from the city of Rome. Tomis
(modern Kustenje) was obviously chosen as a place
Ovid would hate.

Relegatio to Kustenje: the cold salt wind,
treeless and marshbound, on a rocky coast,
scene of an always-renewed humiliation:
this was Ovid's luck.
                    And Dogrose's?

oh, exsilium: he can go anywhere,
blown along like a leaf, he can go anywhere,
like a scrap of orange peel on the restless water,
he can go anywhere,
except to the city.
Dogrose, you long for the city,
                    the city of art,
the ranged towers of fulfilment, the squares
of thought,
the city where all cool poetry is true,
where morning haze melts and everything is seen,
but not wearily, not with hot sanded eyes,
because everything is seen to be in motion,
the motion of a dance, a perpetual arrival:

Dogrose, Dogrose, you have dreamed of this city
but never entered it or heard its murmur,
except sometimes in sleep, or in your art,
when your art happened to be honest and fortunate.

So, Dogrose, your sentence is *exsilium*.

Ovid at least knew the city he longed for:
pacing the cobbles of Tomis, gazing out
with fear and loathing at the frozen marshes,
he could have drawn you, on the spot, a plan

of the city he loved, told you in detail
what everyone was doing at that moment.

stone,
golden stone
warmth-retaining golden stone
sun-quickened warmth-retaining golden stone
noon-polished sun-quickened warmth-retaining golden stone

stairs
cool stairs
seen-through-doorways cool stairs
eye-resting seen-through-doorways cool stairs
impudent eye-resting seen-through-doorways cool stairs

girl
shadowy girl
warmth-retaining shadowy girl
impudent warmth-retaining shadowy girl
seen-through-doorway warmth-retaining shadowy girl

on the sensual stairs
                    noon-polished

bright as the coins that buy her
clinking in my palm

after the wine and the good talk
the hearing of verses.

Yes, I remember the city
and the city's joys
and its golden stones

and I look out across these stiff salt grasses

Relegatio from the known, identified place:
or exsilium in a world of aching gaps,

of spaces where possibility might be, where
voyaging hope might find anything or nothing:

take your choice, and in either case,
and even if you have no choice at all,
go to the top of the main staircase!

        Now the deep Danube
is damned. Winter in the locked heart
of the poet, snow on the salt marshes:
millions of flakes falling on the endless Atlantic,
and on that other Atlantic of grass,
 cruised by mammal ships.
        To the west
of the western landfall. Men know it only
by report. The grass
goes on for ever, and the dark-humped herds
no one can count.

          Ice tinkles in their coats
now, the same ice that rimes the heart of Ovid
(*Whither, unto the bed's foot, life is* shrunk)
The Northern hemisphere endures, endures.
The red man makes a fire of buffalo dung
on the treeless plain (Lee Lubbers, are you there?
The Redskin also has his treasure amid
the unregarded, the carelessly dropped waste).

The great herds move. And with them move the
men,
the women, and the children, and the tents.

> But progress came
> the iron ships came
> the railroads came
> the automatic rifle with
> telescopic sights, came

> If innocence exists
> we see it in that eye
> that patient, shaggy head
> but innocence is air
> through which the bullet flies
> through which the axe-blade falls

> As it fell on the Jews
> as it fell on the gipsies
> innocent, the children
> bewildered as bison calves
> herded into the camps:

> Django, pluck your strings
> for the gipsies who were gassed
> and the gipsies now in England
> herded from their camps
> legislated into despair
> in England now: pluck, pluck
> the taut strings of our hearts.

> And Bill
> will listen a while, and lift
> his belled horn to his lips.
> The buffalo went
> the Indian went
> (to zoos, in either case,
> when they happened to survive)

Well, now it is all over
and the plains have dwindled
to a geographical expression
a certain colour on the map, no more.

I go sometimes to the zoo
to question the buffalo
who never replies

I bend over the railings
as he stands in his pen:
colossal head and round
dark eye remembering what?

Look at a buffalo's eyes some time.
Wide-set, reflecting, round,
the boss of a polished shield

But nothing shielded him.

Francis Parkman in *The Oregon Trail* (1847) describes the life at Fort Laramie, at that time a trading station entirely administered by the American Fur Company, the nearest outposts of the United States Army being seven hundred miles to the east.

The permanent inhabitants of the fort were Indian employees, with a few white supervisors, but it was the rallying-point for Indian tribes on the surrounding plains and a stopping-place for every party of emigrants on their way to Oregon and California. The Dakota Indians, who at that time still felt themselves stronger than the whites, would get wind of the arrival of a wagon-train of emigrants at Fort Laramie, and a whole village would present themselves and demand a 'feast': a cup of coffee and two or three biscuits. Parkman gives an eye-witness account of the arrival of 'Smoke's village' at the same time as that of a wagon-train, and of how Smoke and his people set up their tents on the plain behind the fort, so that a whole Indian village, loud with dogs and children, was suddenly there as if it had arisen from the bare earth.

'One evening about sunset the village was deserted. We met old men, warriors, squaws, and children in gay attire, trooping off to the encampment with faces of anticipation; and, arriving here, they

seated themselves in a semicircle. Smoke occupied the centre, with
his warriors on either hand; the young men and boys came next, and
the squaws and children formed the hems of the crescent. The
biscuits and coffee were promptly despatched, the emigrants staring
open-mouthed at their savage guests.'

Ovid got to Kustenje in the summer
The cobbles sweated. The salt wind
scrubbed the squares with dry heat.
What kind of place is this?
                              Salt marshes,
rocks. Above, Odessa: below, Istanbul,
behind, Bucharest.
                              Half-breed Greeks,
full-blooded barbarians. Shy eyes watching:
'This is the wicked poet sent from Rome,
to live here as a penance.'
                              'A penance? Here?
He'll soon get used to it, if he's a man.'
Unnerved. A few questions. Is this my house?
Are there any books in Latin? Does anyone
speak it, I mean correctly, like a Roman?
Do I sleep on this? Where is my servant?

A fat woman, broad-cheeked, her face secret,
speaking Samatian only.
                              She wipes her hands
ceaselessly on a coarse apron. Her husband
sweeps the courtyard. New shutters will be needed
against the winter.
                              The winter? When will that be?
Not long now. The Danube freezes
for three months. That's when they come.
When who come?
                              That's when they come,
in the winter.
                              They come,
                              They come,

galloping, bows bent.

WHO COME?

Who? What does it matter who?
The ones who always come, to any outpost:
the pitiless fierce riders from out there.

Watch that weather, stranger. When you wake
to find the water in your pitcher frozen,
then one day, soon, you'll hear the drumming hoofs.

That's why we talk so much about the weather.
And why I, too, think of the weather in 1900.
That boy's starved feet cat-quick on the hot bricks.

Burning arrows in the thatch? He makes a home
here?
His hunger makes a home.

Yes, and those streets
in 1900, a boy of six years
walking those streets, thin, his clothes
of the cheapest, nearly worn out
before he got them: but hot
 incitingly hot, under his feet, the brick
pavement, for some reason I always imagine
him in summer, narrow feet
on the hot bricks.
Polluted water
and a towpath with rank
nettles and grass: the thin boy
prowls amid jagged tins. Heat
glares from the blue sky. For some
reason I see him under that hard
blue sky always, smelling polluted
water, watching the smoke
trail its thick arms across, black on blue,
and the bricks hot.

Ah, because
it is my own childhood gives me
my vision of his, the streets were the same
after three decades, the same bricks
held the same heat:
I wandered,
more often in summer than winter,
smelt the canal, was hungry like him,
I mean like him in his inner hunger, I longed
to reach out, to live, beyond these hot
bricks and round black kilns. Home!
I never doubted it, my home was hunger,
that hunger my blood had caught
from his hasty blood.

I see 1900,
trouble in South Africa, volunteers
marching with silver bands down London Road:
I see the thin boy
hungry
always hungry
for food, for life, for the promise that rises
to his narrow feet from the hot bricks.
Where does the canal go? Who reads the signal
poured across the sky by the fat kilns?
Power, money, and trouble:
Wedgwood and Kruger, Spode
and Smuts.
The old queen
turns in her bed and dies. The thin boy,
my father, sees his mother draw the blinds.

The blinds of home. The bailiff has the chairs.
The old queen dies. Grandmother draws the blinds
on the bare dusty room. End of a world.
The kilns go belching on, and Wedgwood
is a liberal MP.

The boy is hungry:
He needs so many kinds of nourishment.
His hunger came to me. I have it still.

Home, home! The narrow houses and the kilns,

The stinking water. The tip above the roofs.
And half a dozen brick town halls.

Why is it always summer in my dream?

Because of the hot sunlight in his eyes?

To speak of exile is to speak of home.
The drumming hoofs across the ice: the poet
listless, far from Rome. Seventy years ago
the smell of the canal and the fat kilns.
The burning arrows crackle in the thatch.
The lost plank floats in the scum-laden water.
The poet shivers. The thin boy dreams of life.

And we speak of home? Of leaving, and returning?
A shake of the dice-box. A cube of time
rolls.

Ovid in Smoke's village. The feathered men
stare at the poet who wrote of one girl
turned to a river, another holding up
arms suddenly twigs and leaves. The plank
in the crushed weeds, inert in that canal,
reared up, hardened to stone, became a dolmen.

Dogrose, *miglior fabbro*, do up your belt:
the muzak ceases and the engines scream.
Back in the airport you were nowhere. Now
on the tarmac, soon at twelve thousand feet,
then at another airport, a bus, an hotel room,
the table and ashtrays of the conference,
still nowhere, always nowhere, and you ask
so piteously, *What am I to do?*

Why, Dogrose, plant a grove of cardboard trees
and walk beneath them in a nylon toga!
the raised plank is
dolmen and totem. Feathered men
file swiftly along the nettled towpath.
Smoke's village pitches camp at Stoke-on-Trent,
smoke's other village.
                                    Dogrose, you seek a theme?
Still want to think and feel yourself a poet?
The dice of time is shaken, rolls and stops.
The Indians and the buffaloes are gone.
Kustenje has no poets, onlyAgitprop.
Pasternak appealed to Krushchev against exile;
his Art of Love was more profound than Ovid's.
After his death, they jailed the one he loved.
The quick thin feet of that boy six years old
have passed across the stones, my friends;
have passed, and will pass, and are passing now.
And Dogrose climbs the international sky.

Music on the Water

to Bill Coleman
in Paris

and like
the river's slow insistence.

In winter, a great padlock. Tugs and strings of
barges
fist-gripped. Summer, a cool flowing.
The sun hatches the shy turtle's eggs.

Sound moves across water:
axe-chop, bow-twang: did the Indians
sing? Or was silence their music?

The river orchestrates silence. It pours.
They looked at it and they said: *Mississippi*.

So time passed, without punctuation.
The river poured and grass waved
in the dateless wind. Red-skinned, high-cheekboned
Adam
named the animals: *opossum*, *chipmunk*.

And sound reached out across water.

But out at sea, the corpses smacked down
into the waves, unweighted.
White bodies were
cheap:
still, a white sailor who died, at least
got cannon-shot at feet and head.

Sick, terrified black bodies
only just worth the cost of carrying
were chucked out if found to be dead
(putrid, not understanding, sick for Africa)
chucked out, like peelings from the galley
to float on the surface till the sharks came up.

Out at sea, the slave ships were coming
Sound reached out across water:
dead-smack of corpse, gull-scream,
chop of the settler's axe, gun-crack and
whip-crack: in the steamy fields
the black backs bend, the long dark song goes up:
the American earth, no longer Eden:
and sound moves out across water.

Africa forgotten,
the hunter's green and yellow beads forgotten,
the snapping apart of the full bean-pod,
the stew simmered with thick yam-flour, forgotten.
The elephant's praisename is Laaye, signifying
'O death, please stop following me':
they forgot the elephant's village-shaking tread
but death did not stop following them.

Voodoo forgotten,
the necklace of teeth forgotten
and the witch-women in coastal areas
with skirts made from octopus tentacles
forgotten also

but the tentacles of misery, the tread
of death broad as the foot of Laaye:
these, they had no occasion to forget.
The Indians were gone
taking with them their music of silence:
now the black backs bent low, and the long dark

song
moved out across the water:

sound of steamboat, of hammer and saw,
of locomotives, of clopping horses
and of the song of sorrowful memory,
the sound of unknown Africa.

And the cobbles of Europe
were already old:
the steep roofs
had kept out many seasons already
the iron cooking-pots of humble men
fed life, humble and recurrent life
stirred by women who bent and dreamed
lay down, rose up and dreamed:

down the slow lanes
the painted wheels were turning, dark-eyed women
crooning old foreign words to their shawled babies

words already old, the language of somewhere
forgotten,
the creak of axles, their home the roadsides of Europe:

En mon pais suis en terre loingtaine

never at home, therefore always at home,
contained,
unspillable:
these were Django's people.
What centuries unwound,
what wars, what exiles, what thunder of surf,
cry of the new-born to the creak of axles,
what bruising of continent against continent,
before the two homeless songs made this their
home:
the plucked string and the quivering mettlesome cry,
the two long journeys meeting here at last.

and Paris in the spring, the cold-eyed spring
hard buds, hard stones
Paris
the cold inexhaustible mother
feeding desire with hard nipples

spring:

time of the dispossessed, the voyagers,
envious only of solitude.

Sweet mother who leaves us all stranded
sweet mother who fuels our veins with hate

under whose bridges we crawl

in the rainy night
amorous as sparrows

the dark flowing Seine
inundating our nerve-centres

And Bill this is your second river
channel of paradoxes
ancient passageway of opposites.

Le sein is a masculine word:
a woman's breasts, masculine! what a race!
crazy inverted logic everywhere!
Le sein is masculine, this is *la seine,*
the drag-net, the bulging tow, the trawl
that disdains nothing, the swag-belly,
full of mussels and contraceptives,
avid of mud, cress and semen,
la Seine, magnet of weightless suicides,
despair of anglers.

The first day, too inert to look for work, I borrowed a rod and went
fishing in the Seine, baiting with bluebottles. I hoped to catch
enough for a meal, but of course I did not. The Seine is full of dace,
but they grew cunning during the siege of Paris, and none of them has
been caught since, except in nets.

> George Orwell,
> *Down and Out in Paris and London.*

A different river, Bill. But the same need.
Something human to make the cold ripples dance.
Something human out of the bell of your horn.

Aching Paris
those spring evenings in big ugly cafes
staring through plate glass at the clicking street
still unaccountably light at eight o'clock
millions of cigarettes fuming like rockets
the girls with alarm clocks ticking between their legs

the pavement sprouting dreams of Martinique
aching Paris, never resting
inexhaustible mother and ticking meretrix,
timed so as to wake us in mid~orgasm
old twisted Paris, gaunt zoo of the poor,
circus ring where the sawdust is milled bone:

Et nous, les os, devenons cendre et pouldre.
De nostre mal personne ne s'en rie;
Mais priez Dieu que tous nous veuille absouldre!

Bill, it is you and only you she needs.
lip those notes! press down those cunning valves!

A thousand years have cropped that sated womb.
Ten centuries of eyesight have blanched the air.
Feet have scrubbed the stones down to dead rubble.

Even the Seine catches nothing but old string.
The European impulse has dried up.
Every seventy years a new lyricism:

She was miraculous! yes, yes, we admit it!
But now, the song-bag is finally sighed out:
different trade-winds are blowing.

Old icy cobbled Paris, twisted streets,
fifteenth century, before the slavers got going,
surf booming innocently on the African beaches
and the university of Paris already two hundred years old:
one of its graduates, bleeding from the face,
well known in that precinct, Francois Villon,
stumbles into the barber's shop, dropping blood.
'Friend, patch me up, I'm leaving.' 'Fighting again?'
His lip is gashed wide open. 'An insolent priest.
I sent him to the other world.'
The barber whistles, dabbing at the wound:
'That'll mean trouble with the authorities.'

Francois de Montcorbier, *alias* des Loges, *alias*
Villon,
(*En mon pais suis en terre loingtaine*)
never from that time a stranger to trouble,
his neck never far from the hempen knot.

Freres humains qui apres nous vivez.
N'ayez les cuers centre nous endurcis

O death, please stop following me

Car, se pitie de nous povres avez,
Dieu en aura plus test de vous mercis

O death, please stop following me
O death, please stop following me

And each continent sang its pure music.

Villon, fugitive, cudgelled, his bones cold,
laughing and singing his crystalline despair,
uttered the pure music of Europe

je meurs de seuf aupres de la fontaine,
Chault commefeu, et tremble dent a dent;
En man pais suis en terre loingtaine;

and under a copper sun
the pure music of Africa rose up:

flight of the egret in words:
repose of the bright parrot among leaves,
lidded pots of clay, woven shields,
quick strut of a disappearing bushfowl:
these things in words:
song, drum and chorus.
The bright feathers fade from the mind,
the hunter's mask, the dance,
feast after hunting, contentment among straw huts,
these fade from the mind:
images pasted over with fear,
fear of the whip, fear of the chain,
of the waves, of the sea-monsters,
of the tossing prison reeking with death:
then forgotten below this, the images,
buried in marrow and blood.

And they also journeyed
the black-eyed people from the forgotten country
painted Romany wheels strained through Europe's
mud

from threat to threat
cursed, harried, their caravans
fired by the soldiery, and the villages
full of hostile eyes at shutters.

From threat to threat they went,
his people, and your people.

And the long journey met at last in Paris:
met, and flowed into music.
Paris, 1935:
the neon lights shone bright
on the dark river
and the epaulettes shone bright
on the shoulders of Hitler's generals
as they bent over maps
their crisscross sights already on Paris
they thirsted for her
the Rhine was mad to flow into the Seine
to die of joy in her grab-net
as a man wants to drive his teeth
into the white shoulders of a girl
those monocled men spread out maps
Paris, Paris, white shoulders
 and behind them, the ovens
already going up
Herrenvolk
must not be jostled in the world's avenues
so build the ovens
Joe Louis knocked out Schmelling
so build the ovens
and build a special one for him.

And in neon Paris, Django strummed
his plangent greeting-chords to life
and your horn was at your lips
and sound moved out, Bill, across the water:

flow, Seine, flow, Mississippi,
flow, strangling Rhine!

Et nous, les os, devenons cendre et pouldre

And I, in by-passed England, rain on the window,
spin your records and groove down the centuries
hearing the creak of axles and the crack of whips
the murmur of women to their shawled babies.

The deep lanes of Europe: the sharks rising
to the unchained corpses: the uncatchable carp
in the *rusée* Seine, knowing all men's tricks:
knowing men to their depths, in the agony
of unillusion, as the whores
know them in the tall, scented houses,
as slaves in their patience know them
unbuttoned, unmasked, yet hung about with
dreams
like mad vines swaying in the tropic night
huge flowers that when we touch them run to scabs.

Bill, my friend, courteous and smiling,
my tall unruffled uncle, at ease in restaurants,
king of the world of easy handshakes,
anchored to Swiss Lily like a bronze statue
on a marble plinth, you know all this:

you and the gipsy Django sang it all.

And now that he is dead, you sing it still.
The night stirs the dark vines, the enslaved eyes
stare on the naked face of pitiable huge Man,

and sound, always your sound, moves out across
the water.

From *Feng* (1975)

[From the author's introduction:

Saxo Grammaticus in Historia Danica tells the story of Horwendil, a governor of Jutland who has a wife named Gerutha, a son named Amleth and a brother named Feng. Horwendil becomes a hero to his people by slaying the King of Norway in single combat; Feng, in jealousy, murders him, marries his queen and ascends his throne. Finally Horwendil's murder is avenged by Amleth, who clouds his purpose under a disguise of madness.

The story has been rehandled several times, notably by Shakespeare and Laforgue, but these rehandlings concentrate mainly on the character of Amleth; my version is concerned with Feng, the sick and hallucinated person who seizes power and then has to live with it. Since I have lived through an age in which raving madmen have had control of great and powerful nations, the theme naturally seems to me an important one.]

A Circle of Stones and a Nude Blade

I, the he that is I, shall be king. The crowning
is solemn. Stones in a circle
ranged roughly, with rude veneration
signify strength: in vain the sea-borne
storms hammer their humped shapes: all heroes
would wish for this weight, unmoved by winds.
No chisel changed them: only man's choice
set them apart from peers, and portaged
to stand in a circle – his species' signature
in that rounding only, no rune written.
Men are mist, so runs their message,
waving reeds, wraiths seen through rainbows,
a wolf's howl in the windy forest,

no stay and no standing, but we stones
endure, without end, the weather's envy.

King-crowning is toward. And the crooked Feng
is made straight. Stone-circled, at sunrise
the waiting warriors shall see their will
dourly enacted, their deeming demonstrated:
saluting the king, their stern selection.
Me they have chosen, the changer Feng,
whose sudden poison, in that passage poured,
altered all attitudes: like a wild anagram
spelt the world sideways. Now I am spilt:
the old wine wasted, the new water
not yet poured, the pristine vessel
too cracked to contain it, in any case.

Notice that I have no punishing nightmares,
no sense of sin, slayer of brother:

Horwendil's life? An heroic hog
whose blood ran into a bucket? He blundered
from combat to combat, kingly killer
admired by adherents, his ethics archaic.
If life is numinous, he never knew it.
All sense of the sacred escaped his scope
and theirs who today think of his thews,
look round for a link, a likelihood
of continuing kingship, a strong foe-crusher:
to forbid strangers, to fight sternly,
to fell trees for fortress, the flowing river
to dam for defence, to aim death
at armoured opponents, these were his offices.
Now, of me they demand them. His death-dealer
but in secret. Still, even if stoutly
I got up and growled that I had gutted
their snoring hero, snuffing his heart-flame
by stealth as he slept, they would be startled
no more than a moment: then, matter-of-fact
as becomes brain-bashers, they would rise and beat

shields in applause. The alert attacker
deserves to prevail: the prone, paunch-full
fool was fair fodder.
So they would feel,
and I feel nothing. A new numbness
blankets my bones, betrays my brain.
Am I altered? Am I the other?
The insinuator, whose agents infiltrated
the castle of my caring? My conscious flowing
was always elsewhere: the shy animals,
patient or pouncing, were my preceptors.
Did I for a moment metamorphose, mouthing
liquid death like a snake, or leaving on lawn
no more than a ferret's footprint? By favour
of beasthood did I shed that brother-burden?

If so, I learnt the wrong lesson. My longing
was the falcon's freedom, the fish-hunting
heron's stance, his stilted silence,
the coney's casualness in coming and going.

But this? the stark circle, the starved sun
shaping thin shadows, the sharp rim
of gold at my temples, the gruff greeting
of warriors who witness their will's working?

And after, what? The weary wind
that blows through a life of bone and metal?
the talk of war, torment of women
and chiller of children? For ever to choke
on the cold breath of death-vows, the voice of
vengeance?

AH, BUT, I interrupt the march of metrics, tapping myself on the
unaccustomedly bardic shoulder, do not forget that when you stepped
into Horwendil's piteously cramped shoes and offered your brow to
his egregiously irksome crown, automatically and *ipso facto* slid

between the warmed sheets of his bed. Yes, Gerutha, the queen and therefore the property of the king, except in the case of a king already married, is standing with demure and bridely mien at your side. Thus I admonish myself. Still young, still fair, mother though she be of the tall Amleth with hooded, accusing eyes. There, beside me, she stands. For somehow, the fevered and confused foreboding has become the event itself, the intervening hours have gone by like a sick dream and I am actually here, now, in the centre of the ring of stones. In the presence of the elder warriors (for our rough coastal society, intent on plunder, does not rise to a priesthood, not feeling the need for any formal contriving of a channel between the Here-and-Now and the Out-There), I become king, I become Gerutha's husband.

> Fair-haired and creamy of flesh, certainly wise
> to the sensual trade-routes, generous of thighs
>
> and breasts, she belongs now to me by right
> and I dread the slow coming-down of the wedding night
> and by this recoil I know myself human
> the animal that rejects and prefers. Woman
>
> to man makes biological sense
> our need for the blind spasm is as intense
>
> as that of dog-fox and vixen in the covert
> why then are we hesitant and introvert?
>
> I do not know why, I only know that the lust
> I should feel for this convenient mate is trussed
>
> in with my lame will and cannot break free
> that tonight when I should be topping her blithely
>
> shall draw back, into silence and darkness, alone
> and where there should he life and flesh there will be
> ghost and bone
>
> and I who have always tried to learn from the untamed
> beasts of the forest and mountain am stopped and
> ashamed

finding myself powerless even to turn the pages
of the great book they read effortlessly through the ages:

they obey one great energising law, *Be as you have been:*
instinct moves them onward through the unchanging
scene

and like a crest of surf that never comes to the beach
it ferries them on their complicated errands, each

adept at an incredible variety of skills
defended by hypertrophied senses against all ills

intended to them by foes equally organised
or against hazards of dearth and disease, every sized

and shaped calamity. Their compulsion is so graceful
and so simple, it makes our clutter of choices seem
wasteful:

they go at once where they have to go, do what is
indicated:
how shall our endless chopping and changing be vindicated?

Is it I who am free, and the animals enslaved
to their rigid patterns, those unbreakable laws engraved

on their nervous systems, so that to disobey
cannot occur to them? I, whose dismay

at this fertile and comely den-partner no bear
or wolf would agonize? The whale, in search of air

breaking the surface, then in search of food
cruising subaqueous, knows there is a good

beyond air and food, but where I can say I *am lonely*
he has no formulated concept of need, he knows only

that something keeps him swimming when he would
otherwise float
at rest, warm-blooded in his glutinous snug coat:

nor, in all that cold water, is his great penis
likely to extend itself without some ectaccan Venus

to offer immediate prospect of immolation
(how unlike mine! which, apt to desert its station

when ordered to attack, at times when nothing is doing
so often signals an impulse to go a-wooing).

Yes, the animals shame us. Complete in their present tense
how they must despise our abashed time-ridden existence
content with the simple energy and the simple good
they do not fear old age or yearn back to childhood
and when death comes at last to impose its Then
on their unthinking Now, they do not, like men,

suffer agonies of regret for what they failed to do
or care how they will be remembered. Life is new
and so is death, their memories do not retain the old
except for the ancestral pattern in the neural mould:
but here am I....

Here am I indeed, lost in these thoughts, abstracted from what, for
everyone else present, is a moment of fierce actuality. The warriors
with their barbaric horn-helmets and their heavy moustaches,
clanking at each movement with their cherished instruments for
bone-cracking and blood-releasing, are staring up curiously at the king
they have just chosen. They wait for words from me.

I utter a short martial speech, prepared in advance, in which I paint
an utterly false picture of myself as a being devoted to violence and
conquest. I represent myself as caring deeply for territorial expansion.
It is, I tell them, the supreme object of my life that this backward tribe
of littoral-dwellers, deficient in every skill except the murder of
human beings and animals, fog-brained bipeds who have not yet
evolved a philosophy even in its chrysalis form, a religion – that these
anthropoid allosaurs should he armed, organised and encouraged to
hurl themselves on other similar groups, scattered thinly along a
coastline which provides already more than enough timber, fish and
arable ground to meet their needs for a thousand years, and, to the

accompaniment of much brain-spattering and windpipe-severing, deprive them of their habitat and their clutter of unenviable possessions.

Having told this pack of lies, and gained at any rate the appearance of assent from them, I turn my attention to the female partner of my predicament. Taking her unresisting hand in mine, I declare that she is my queen, and that I shall show her my loving respect by the traditional means of sleeping for the first three nights with a naked sword in the bed between us. This usage is intended to convey that the bride-groom is not simply grabbing at this bride out of blind lust, that he is prepared to restrain his desires until she has grown used to his presence.

Gerutha smiles, indicating that she appreciates the traditional compliment, and at the same time side-glancing at me to let me know that she is ready when I am.

Down from the stones. Leave them behind, to the wind and rain, to the call of ravens and the silent growing of the grass.

And then, of course, the wedding-feast. What else?
The drinking, and the boasting. The thick air
shimmers with male display: virility,
aggressiveness. Unsatisfactory gods.

The queen and I retire to rest, before
bone-throwing starts. Some will be killed tonight.
I do not want to see. There will be time
for killing. And, perhaps, for nothing else.

I killed to rid myself of Horwendil.
And now I find that I have killed myself.
For I am Horwendil and he is dead.

Gerutha's maids disrobe her. And my page
unbuckles belts, and pulls off boots. The sword?
There is, it seems, a ritual for this.
The appropriate servant brings it. Down the middle
of the soft bed he lays it, and the correct
word-spell is uttered. Old retainer, he
did the same office for our father once.

He bows. The other servants bow. They leave.
Gerutha lies on her side of the blade.
I lie down too. It is a ritual sword,
not sharp at all. I could reach over it
and touch her skin, or take her hand in mine.
I touch the sword instead. I think it is
safer to touch the metal than the flesh –
the infertile metal, hammered clean of feelings
before it reached me, than the throbbing flesh:
deluded, hot with need, crowded with ghosts.
And now at last I am the king I killed.

Feng Meditates on the Madness of Amleth

Suppose a man in the squid-haunted gloom of his mind
says, *I will worship the sea and only the sea,*

or climbing the steep rock to the granite cell
says, *I will worship the stone and only the stone,*

the world to him would vibrate in that music
all would be tested by the water or by the stone

as the penguin's eye sees only the colour of cold.

What did Horwendil worship? What filled his eye?
Was it the veined earth of Jutland, the dark cliffs

of seaward granite and the cold rivers?
Or was it enough to sport and wallow in

Gerutha's milk and roses? And does Amleth
ramble in the thwart moonrise for love of Horwendil?

Can madness make its own sea-shores and mountains?

My counsellors say Amleth's madness is a mask:
behind it his revenge-thoughts grow cool as cress.

And a mask, what is that? Is it ivory or carved stone
or the immobile features of a bird of prey?

In winter, my soldiers can stamp in solid armour
across the surface of the deepest lake:

yet the water is there. The ice is its clouded mask.
Is Amleth's madness the water, or the ice?
Does his nature lap hungrily under that cold lid,

needing my helpless bulk netted in the weeds,
needing the sweet flavour of my rotting flesh?

Are his thoughts the fish that grieve not for empty skulls
the thin fish that dart through eye-holes?

Or are they placid under the ice-tent of reason?

As for me, my madness is to be sane.
With my head on Gerutha's pillow, trying not to dream

that Amleth's dark girl has me in her fastness
and that the orchard bees have left off buzzing.

My insanity is to be the cold king
with the curtains of his mind drawn tight together,

sitting at counsel with shadows, talking to ghosts.

From *New Poems 1978-79*

Visiting an Old Poet

As I walked from the village to his house
along that curving half-mile of road, I thought,
it's twenty-two years. And I almost turned back.

But when I came through the door, and saw him
sitting on the sofa in the long cool room
and he looked up, and smiled, and knew me, I thought
This will be good. And at once came the next thought,
not separate, two blossoms on the one spray,
It would be fitting to make a poem for him.

I knew he was old.
Everyone knows it. His oldness has become
the chief thing they know about him: *old, old, old.*
Most of the people who run the world,
who run the publishing houses, the studios,
the news agencies, the people who pay your fare
to go and see him and write something interesting
they were not born and their parents were not born,
when he was young and stubborn and full of sap
and running over with poetry, when he was savage
sarcastic and funny, when he cut rough capers
across respected graves with waxen lilies
under domes of glass: splintering the domes,
breaking the pale wax petals.
Oh Lord of life,
where were you keeping them, the not-yet-born,
back in the days of his youthful sun and rain?

Were they full of hope, little half-formed bat-souls
beating their leather wings against the glass
to get into the lighted, scented world?
Or were they torpid at the end of the cave,
hanging in clusters, unwilling to come down,
feeling secure as long as their hooked claws

held on to the rough cold roof?
Did they ever want
the world as it is, with all its wheeling fires
and exploding stars?
                       But he wanted it, he
ran forward, sometimes crazed with panic,
sometimes falling headlong and covering his eyes
because of the terror of the living world:
but always rising again when the fit had passed,
climbing shakily first to his knees
then, gasping, to his feet, an upright man,
a man silhouetted against terror and joy.

So I entered the house and I saw his body
sitting where it had sat two decades before,
in the same stance, or only a little slackened:
in the same clothes, or the same kind of clothes.

It was his soul, of course, that I wanted to touch –
his vibrant, feeling web of inner truth:
not prod and poke it like a farmer, nor
assess it knowingly like an auctioneer,
but gently and respectfully question it,
and receive some rays of its light, some particles of its warmth,
so long as I was not robbing him of strength,
not draining his spirit. (I need not have worried.
His strength is not less than it always was,
though in some ways it is different.) Approaching his soul
I had to walk down the avenue of his body,

or rather clamber that rock-strewn mountain pass
where one can see the marks of old violences –
the whitened bones of animals and men,
and giant trees snapped off by bounding rocks:
for this, in the thawing season, was avalanche country.
And so I touched his body, and spoke to it
(Once, after a silence, he put his hand on mine.
It felt like just-dried clay. And he said 'Cold.')

So of course as we sat together I asked myself,
What is it, then, to talk with a man's body?

Is the body a shell?

Is the body a highway?

What is the body, is it a cave
where the soul goes to get messages?

Perhaps that is it, perhaps it is a cave
where the soul knows a word will be spoken,
either by the sybil who lives at the far end of the cave
or by the god of freedom who now and then
puts his handsome bearded face into the cave
softly laughing, and then speaking a word:
or not speaking at all, just dancing for a moment
in the casual likeness of a jet of water.
Or perhaps some wild animal who has crept
into the cave for shelter, in adversity,
hunted, or pinched by a hard frost,
will crouch behind a rock somewhere in the cave
and utter a cry, and the cry will come out as a word:
and the soul will hear it as a word,
and understand, and come out satisfied:
will leave the cave of the body, quietened,
satisfied and answered.

Notice that I do not ask what the soul is.
(Ah there, Walt! You invented this idiom,
this kind of talking and questioning in a poem:
and you were an old poet, too, in time,
and people visited you in Camden, New Jersey:
ah there, Walt! I have always loved you too.)
Notice, I say, that I do not ask what the soul is,
everybody knows that, it is too obvious.

The soul is not an entity but a process.
It is a state of accepting and co-ordinating:
the pattern of a dance when the limbs that were dancing
have sunk to rest, the toss of a green bough
in the wet spring wind, after the tree has fallen:
the flutter of a white handkerchief waved in farewell,
when the handkerchief is folded and put away:
the pattern, the toss, the flutter, these go on,
and these are the soul. Everyone knows that.

Age, in its bodily manifestations, arouses our pity,
when the sinews shorten and cramp, the muscles dissolve,
eyesight and hearing dim, movement is vague:
but age I find not pitiable in fulfilled men.
It completes the triumphal arch of their life.

For this poet, it is not his eight decades
or not they only, that make the condition of age,
but the stillness that has fallen upon his mind
as gently as snow while the brain was hushed in sleep
and the eyes were not looking.
When they opened again
to the light, and the brain renewed its registering,
the stillness had come, the man at last was old.
Now decisions are made only by the body's declension.
He listens only to the susurrus of time
who once heard the eagle's shriek from the farthest mountain,

the most distant rasp of the shy raven,
the vixen's scream in the darkest of thickets
Where once he moved towards change as a feeder of life
now he waits for the change that moves towards him.
But the waiting has its richness too: in patience
and in fulfilment it hears its own clear music,
a music for the accepting spirit to dance to,
making sense of the movement of his feet

as it was then, and as it had to be,
long years ago, and yesterday, and now.
It was not senseless wandering after all.
It was a dance, across a patterned floor.
The music rounds it out: he hears, and sees.

*

His poems bloom around him, flowers
planted with the seed of his fresh hours.

He set them in the ground to bloom
when he was strong and desirous as a bridegroom.

Now his strength has left him, but theirs
is always renewed in colours and fragrant airs.

At rest amid an energy he no longer needs
he breathes calmly while all urgency recedes.

He is patient as a statue of rained-on stone.
There will be no more poems now the bird has flown,

the magic bird that came and went silently
scattering poem-seeds from the cloud-dappled sky.

But he does not grieve, he no longer needs the bird,
content to wait now for the one unknowable word

to form in the cool silence of his stilled brain:
the human songs are over, earth's loss is heaven's gain,

or the gain of whatever it is lies ahead
across the gulf of death, when the old skin is shed,
and the one unknowable word is finally said.

So far, my unambitious poem has crept
close to the ground: the rhythms of talk, and easy
rhymes. But enough. Rise, winged horse! Fly, Muse!
Soar nearer to your subject, give strain for strain,
paean for paean. You celebrate a singer,

not of shanties or cool cabaret ditties, but
a robed singer, a lofty builder, a patient carver
of masks for the great truths!

*

I think of his life. Divagations enough:
from many vessels he slaked the one deep thirst:
passion and the need for passion were his themes:
his heart's goal was the never-remaining moon,
he lived by day in the light of his night's dreams:
the same sacred madness in the last as in the first,
the immortal garment woven from mortal stuff

Each straight-backed and fine-nostrilled youthful queen
hair of raven's wing or of cornfield
paused in her dancing when he spoke the needful word
halted amid the shine of the travelling moon
in homage to his need as still as a stone bird
against ripple of water and a sky where stars wheeled:
as if his hunger for her was the first truth she had seen.

How shall we see this need? With pity? A common man's itch?
Many would deny it the crown and title
of love, which they say takes root and holds, holds
and is the only constant thing beneath the moon.
But surely passion, which unweariedly gives and unfolds
finding in each queen beauties beyond recital
is love as we know it, or something just as rich:

on hot summer days, in the woods, I have often waited
amid calm thickets where light was an emerald slant
with hope, sometimes fulfilled, to hear the nightingale
who seeks the day's green tent and the night's clear moon:
and surely I loved when, shy and hidden as a snail,
I listened with wonder to the sudden divine descant
from the small feathered throat, a bird not separated

from nightingale-nature, sharing its bird-delight
with man-delight, or rather not caring
what becomes of the notes once they have been released
into the green calm. And it is the one moon
he gives fealty to, though her form has never ceased,
to round or slim as she sails through the dark, never wearing
the same shape twice nor the same fullness of light

If I, entranced listener, love one nightingale
as much as another, since the music is the same,
so he has loved women. Can I feel surprise
that he, whose map of truth is the face of the moon,
should have loved moon-nature and woman-nature in
whatever guise
they chose to appear? His fire was one constant flame,
though fuelled by the changing female and the changing male.

*

'He has no memory.' Sequence matters less
when you are living in an endless now.
What did he have for breakfast? Which
breakfast – today's or the one that ended his childhood,
 that morning when he stood, in a sharp collar,
by a family fireplace suddenly grown strange,
packed, labelled, waiting for the station cab
to go to school and eat and sleep with strangers
for ever and ever? Or the breakfast he carried
to his first bride on their first waking-up

in their own rumpled bed? (He timed the eggs
in the sunny kitchen, drunk with her shadowed hair.)
Which breakfast? The stiff rashers he chewed and gagged on
waiting beside the fire-step, under the sandbags
with dawn staining the sky, and bayonets fixed
and every man's face drawn to a mask of death,
Which breakfast did he eat today? He lives
beyond the reach of time as it reaches me.
Sequence? What is it but an arrangement of time?

And time in itself is nothing: a neutral accretion.

Time is an emptiness that acknowledges
it must be filled somehow, with some nature.

Last night I smelt the air that moved across
the meadows, after a long day's sun
on ground that had been soaked. The grass and flowers
flavoured the air, and the breath and harmless dung
of the slow-moving animals. I breathed, and my breath
was prayer.
Yet the air was just air. And time is just time. Sometimes I see it as a
clear liquid
waiting to be tinctured by a drop of thought.
There are red thoughts, and purple thoughts, and green
thoughts,
and thoughts of slate colour, waiting to colour time.
The transparency of time is offensive to nature:
it is more, it is a contradiction,
it is forbidden by the law of the universe.
There is no such thing as the clear liquid time.
That is what time would be if left to itself,
but it is not left to itself.
I say time is thought.
Without thought it is forbidden to exist.
Even the rocks and pools have consciousness.

Clay and sand think in their calm fashion.
Much more the plants, more still the animals,
most of all we who are walking dream-cages.

To think about anything is to change its nature.
A new thing, that has never been thought about
exists over-simply in its two dimensions.
It needs to impinge, and to be thought about.

Our dog sleeps on an old blanket. He twitches
and growls, then breathes softly. When the blanket was new
it was just a folded blanket in a warehouse.
Then it was bought and carried to a bed,
where it kept people warm while they slept or talked,
or made love or quarrelled. And sometimes while they died.
In its old age it slid from bed to floor.
We gave it to him when he was a puppy,
to reassure him when he was left alone.
He needed it then because it smelt of us:
now, it smells of him.
The blanket is time,
and time is the breath and growl of the sleeping dog,
and the people making love and keeping warm,
and quarrelling, and letting the blanket slip
from bed to floor. Time is sweat, and thought, and kisses.

The sequence does not matter. Time is a cube.
If it happened once it is still happening.
The dog sleeps while the couple kiss and the man dies:

the creak of the mattress as the dying man
stiffens for the last time with open sightless eyes
is the same creak as when he lays her down.
And the dog groans, 'It all happens for ever.'
He lays his ears down flat and sleeps again.

*

So I encountered his body. This was not trivial.
It was still upright and convivial.

His body moved slowly. Inside it, soul stirred.
I touched the cage bars and looked in at the bird

Facing him, I came back once more to that question:
does soul follow body's every suggestion,

or is body the servant, the snarling Caliban,
feeling cheated without soul, feeling less than a man,

so that soul must be renewed in him over and over?
(Yet renewal's true spring and source he can never
 discover.)

You could plot this poet's life by his body's story,
the steps by which soul climbed to its last promontory.

*

Three times his body lived. In youth, it fought:
knew death: survived: in fecund middle years
it loved and nurtured, calming children's fears
and rousing women to its strength. Such thought

sustained him till the blood past action cooled.
And then his body slept. In dreams it moved
towards the souls and bodies it had loved,
thence to the knowledge-grove where dreams are schooled.

Who taught our blood to seek out answering blood
coursing in rhythms that complete our own,
he asked: did body? soul? or some high rnage

licensed by God to marrow lifeless bone
with energy? What master found it good
to flood us with love's rage that seeks love's rage?

I, poet caught in sharp cross-winds of trouble
visited a poet at rest among his harvest's stubble
His field was reaped and the full sheaves were in the barn
May frost and mildew never come to do them harm.
May his last days be bright and calm as this June evening
and when death comes may it glide on level wing:
and may he, who made life's grit into pearls for a necklace
teach me always that art should be considered but life
reckless.

[The old poet, of course, is Robert Graves, whom John Wain went to see on Majorca in the late 1950s and was asked again to interview for a national newspaper a few years before he died.]

Enobarbus

I'm grizzled now. A skull packed with memories. When I was young,
if anyone had said
Where does your strength come from? I'd have laughed.
Where does anything's strength come from? Shoots
push from the warm earth: even desert sand,
given one shower of rain, grows green with seed
that must have been hiding somewhere.
Frogs
leap twelve times their own length, birds climb the wind,
the lion rips open the gazelle's hot flank.
And I, Enobarbus, Red-beard,
have shoulders to support plated armour
a spine to stand upright with a loaded pack,
legs hard for the Alpine passes, a hand
that can squeeze a man's life out of his throat
if his studded shield has broken my sword.
Sea and the rocks are strong. I am strong.
Soldier-strong, Enobarbus-strong:
a man born to lift armies off the earth
and press them backwards to surrender and death:
that's what I'd have said.

> All strength comes from the sun. I knew that.
> But I had not learnt
> what it means to know that.

> All strength reaches down
> from
> the gold-bossed, impersonal
> all-giving, staring, unrecognising
> indifferent
> sun.

The sun that warms
carrion for maggots
burnishes the dead moon
tortures to death the lost
soldier in the desert
tunes the throats of birds
in February

the sun
the sun
this I had not yet learnt:

till I saw Antony.

After that
I saw the oak-tree's strength
locked in the acorn.

Only the sun has the key.
Only the sun has my key.

*

Everyone said he was like Hercules.
What is it for a man to be like a god?

Gods are all round us, like air.
They are under our feet, like earth.

We drink them, we breathe them, we
hear them, we know them:
we forget them like the things we know best.

We eat them
so their strength becomes ours
it is the only strength we have

gods have long green limbs
and flowers for faces

and gesturing leaves for hands
gods have heads of spray
 and smooth dimpled skin
rock-rounding
gods have rough pelts and bucking hems and genitals of flame

gods have
gods have
and sometimes they give it sometimes to one of us

*

That winter when he took us through the Alps ...

Enobarbus remembers the Alps

The mountains never think of death. Or life
Their huge white heads are turned the other way,
their sharp stone teeth bared to the sharper air.

He carries full pack and spear
like the rest of us. His shoes
squeak on the snow like ours.
That's in the morning, when
we start to climb. By noon
the sun glares from hot blue: we're frying
in our own grease. His shield
throws back hard yellow at the sun.
For God's sake rest the men.
They're starving: some are struck
with snow-blindness, have to put their hands
on the others' shoulders.
Suck ice,
he says, it will at least fill your stomachs with clean water. And
march.

Snow-heads that cannot think of death are turned

away from life. Huge teeth grin at the sky.
They can not care. They can not know. Can not.

March. Suck ice. There will
be rations waiting on
the downward side. Two days.
It is forbidden to die
before then. Suck ice. March.

The snow squeaks in the morning. Later
it is slush. Laden men splash
and slip. When the sun goes
behind those snow-heads and stone
teeth, the night will pounce. We
shall be loaded with skin-peeling
chains of ice.
A goat's bones
lie scattered. It must have starved,
weakened, and fallen kicking from a crag. Its burst
skeleton, cleaned white by crows,
lies close by our path. Everyone
sees it. Everyone thinks
of his own weakening, his own
fall, his own wrecked skeleton.
Nobody speaks, nobody wants
to hear his own voice say,
'starvation' or 'goat'.

And that thing he ate!
It must have been the corpse of
a marmot, or something.
The smell made me puke.
But he ate it, standing up:
'I must have strength,' he said calmly.
That's how he went through the Alps.
That's how he went through battles.
That's how he went through women.

Cleopatra? Yes, very beautiful.
Did I what?
Well, of course,
I know the answer you're expecting.
But funnily enough, no, I didn't
fantasize about her.
I followed
him around, in most things, but
not that far.
                        Whenever
he was in there, after dinner, undressing her,
getting up to all those tricks (the slaves
used to spy on them, we all
knew everything): even on those hot nights
when I would lie in my tent, feeling
randy enough for anything, sweating,
trying not to masturbate because
I wanted to be fresh next day, even then: no.
It's as if my body knew
she was for him, not me.
Oh, she was every bit as beautiful
as they say. And *une grande*
horizontale. Look, I know sex
when I see it. Yet what burned in her
wasn't just sex. It was that and
something else.
What else? Well,
I can't find words for it. You know those fish
with **a** phosphorescent spine? This – something – lit
her up
all through her shape, like that.
To Antony,
she was just another woman in the end.
That's because his magic equalled hers.
To me, she was always music, a dance,
colour, a skin of wine, the seasons

on a base of woman.
And sex? That big
erection she's supposed to have given the men just by walking past?
I don't care
whether you believe or not, I never had it.
And yet, well
what I felt for her was never chaste:
it was close to lust. Close to it, but different.
I don't know how to put it. I would have liked
to do something to her, something bold
and very intimate, yet not quite sexual:
such as, for instance, licking her armpits.

Yes, that would have satisfied me.
Or driven me mad for ever. Enough now.

Cleopatra was

the red vein in a smooth
white pebble

Cleopatra was

a voice from down among the cluster
of houses by the waterfront

singing the same song
over and over

on one of those nights when you can't sleep
a song with the richness of tears

Cleopatra was

a hot jet of goat-sperm

Cleopatra was

a winged seed fluttering down,

taking a long time to reach the ground

Cleopatra was

the lace of cloud that moves
past the staring moon

Cleopatra was

the sparkle of salt on the stiff ropes
of a fishing boat

when it rests in the sun, and the men
who fought the sea's fury, rest
in the calm of the sun, and drink wine

Cleopatra
was

*

In the brief dusk they heard it
when swallows wheel
for the last time before resting
for the last time before their quick heart-beat
composes to sleep in cups of mud and straw
still beating fast in sleep
but not caring, not seeking, not needing, quiet
in the warmth of clay and stone:

in the brief dusk
when the sky turns cool
when the light turns green
in the silent time
before the frogs in the hot night
before the owls
before the long yell of the wild dog
before the song from the taverns:
as the swallows wheel for the last time
the soldiers heard it:

his music of desolation.
They listened and fear struck them
they listened and sorrow bowed their heads
they listened and could not speak.

Later, pale and quiet-voiced
they told us of it:

the music under the ground
in the motionless air
among the tranced limbs of trees
the music of desolation:
the good-bye music.

What god left him?
Hercules, king of war
or Bacchus, ruler of feasts?
they asked each other.
What god loved him most?

In the brief dusk
they were afraid of the green light.

Who cares what god left him?
It was music of ending:
the lithe wings folding back,
the rustle of their closing.

When a man's luck gives out
he hears that music in his skull
in the brief dusk:
who cares what god makes it?
No more of questions and answers.
The great sun drops down.
The swallows have nested.

*

Enobarbus reasons with Subrabone

I lie here in the soft, stifling darkness
staring straight up at the roof of my tent.
Rain is falling, the ropes should be slackened.

Enobarbus

Look, try to understand. Soldiering is a profession. You
don't open a shop with nothing to sell. And you don't
write a book nobody is going to read. Unless you're mad.
And I'm not mad. The only point of fighting is to win.
Striking attitudes, making fine speeches, throwing your
life away, they're for amateurs.

Subrabone

> If it is over, strike your tent and move.
> He has nothing to hold you but the chains of love.

Enobarbus

He can't win. His luck has run out. Not that I really
believe in luck: that's the point. A professional knows
how to stay sane. He weighs the chances and goes in at
the right time, in the right place, with the right men and
equipment or else he doesn't go in at all.

Subrabone

> You think it folly to have served so long?
> A great defeat can ring like a great song.

Enobarbus

He's a madman. That's what she's made of him. Everyone
who was there knows I tried my best. I knew if someone
didn't pry him loose from her he'd sooner or later be a
dead duck. Wefl, now it's happened. He's finished.

Subrabone

> It is not your small thoughts make you
> faint-hearted
> but that still music as the loved god departed.

Enobarbus

He's finished but is that any reason why I should be
finished with him? Where's the sense in that, where's
the justice? It's not as if I were betraying my country.
This is a quarrel between Romans. A sane Roman
against a mad Roman. All I'm doing is crossing the fines from
Roman to Roman, from the mad to the sane, it's my
duty. An experienced soldier is an asset to the Empire.
If I stay with Antony I'll be as much use as a slaughtered
pig hanging up beside a stall with a hook through one
foot. Not even that much use because I'm no good to
eat. I'd be no prettier to look at and I'd be just as dead.

Rain, rain. Where's my orderly? Asleep
or drunk? The ropes should be slackened, fool,
the ropes should be slackened. The ropes
should be slackened.

And now at last I am
alone in my nerve-ends

unable to call his name
or any name

houseless, a sound
'Enobarbus'

no self, no possibility
of touching another

and now at last I am
insubstantial

my suchness
blown to a mist

tales of my courage
a scarf of mist

my jove-scattering sex
mist over the ditched fields

smoke from a guttering candle
in a socket of solitude

and now at last I am
and now at last
and now
and

FROM *SHORTER POEMS 1970-1978*

'Your beauty chokes me.
Colour, shape, all'

Your beauty chokes me. Colour, shape, all,
But chokes me into peace. My conflicts die
Like clouds that shred into a perfect sky.

I hope yours do the same, who give so much.
One truth at least I know: when we lie down
You shiver into pleasure at my touch.

I never can deserve you: still, I try.
What can I give you, but this Bacchanal?
The bill is waiting, and we must go Dutch.

But oh the radiant smile behind time's frown!

Oh forest where the flimsy shoots grow tall!
Oh clean and salty ocean where we drown!

Czech Students in Oxford, Seen Across a Room, 1968

It is always summer in his dream of home:
the wheat scarcely ripe, and the swallows
coming in low for insects.

That was the summer of the brimming river
when the grasshoppers chirped like choristers:
vespers and matins in a new dialect!

Now, home is a tangle of roots.

Now, he wakes to the dark mornings
Frost has made hardware of the earth:
its veins cold as the forgetful tracks of tanks.

Fall, snow, fall, weightless snow
from the mothering sky:
conceal the biding roots where life is gathered,
the rune-dark roots whose names are his only prayers.

To My Young Self

I remember you so well, lank~haired restless one.
Shall we attempt a dialogue at last?

If I could roll up three decades like a worn carpet,
and walk with you among these trees,

or in this lane by the old blackened wall,
where your starveling footstep often came,

among these scenes that keep the same outline,
it might calm both of us.

After all, we came through it together,
you changing slowly into me.

Came through what? Ah, diablotin,
we both know how jagged was the path

and how our joint footfall altered its nature:
becoming heavier, more poised, less free.

You wandered in a hailstorm of choices,
each choice numbered and coloured like snooker.

Decisions, choices, possibilities,
rolling on the green cloth of your life.

One by one they disappeared into pockets.
now only a few are left to invite collision.

I chalk my cue for the shots that will decide the game.
I need skill, where you needed only appetite.

Cadaverous joker, the feelings that shook your
bones

and broke your health, were in fact your best
friends.

Your voice echoed among Easter Island heads:
mine shouts along a valley littered with broken
waxworks.

You had to break iron bars to get out:
I have to unpick silken ropes to stay out.

Nothing could help you but the stubbornness to
live.
Nothing can help me but the stubbornness to live.

The word led you upward into a mountain
landscape.
The word leads me downward to the banks of a
strong river.

You were in danger of falling and being broken.
I am in danger of sinking and being engulfed.

But after all, we are the same person, gallowglass,
both the same timorous but untrainable animal:

more easy under the cold sky than in a kennel,
rooting for bitter grubs, not waiting to be fed
mince.

You with the wild laughter and the apprehensive
eyes,

wondering where the next smash on the nose
would come from:

I, knowing by this time just where it will come
from:
no longer laughing like a madman, my eyes calmer.

Well, I have enjoyed our talk together,
though I admit I did most of the talking

and found it rather difficult to draw you out:
but then I am fifty-one, and you are what? twenty?

twenty-one, twenty-five? in any case, bambino,
though I do not suppose you trust me, I will trust
you,

having not much else to trust, and no patrimony
save the few battered belongings that used to be
yours.

'Outside, gulls squabbled in the empty street'

Outside, gulls squabbled in the empty street. Criticism
and name-calling. Salt air scrubbed the gleaming
Sunday morning walls. Gutter-split stalks, leaves, fuelled the
squalling
and wheeling. Feet, motors, slept. The inured citizens
turned over to snore again. Beside me, my darling

slept in a deeper peace, like a princess in a fable
all through the sea-clean, gull-torn dawn, slept below
dreaming,
stunned by those hours of outrageous bliss, bliss upon bliss,
when love leapt higher than even the fiercest lovers were able.
Patient, I lay, expecting tea and her morning kiss.

Evening over the Place of Cadfan

Over again, these gifts: the high bareness:
the spear-grass, the sheep carved in stone
watching me pass, the darkening granite
still dabbed with lyric green. And at my back
the levelled-off tips dead quiet, these man-made cliffs
too surgical for grass, human work to the end,
but work of departed giants, all that determination
signed off for ever, the hubbub of silenced voices:
after such purpose, nothing but loneliness, wildness:
and out at sea,
the day's sun in his lead coffin.

Rhosgadfan, Gwynedd
1975

In the Beginning

Now, in our perfect hour,
while the green stem supports the weightless
flower,
before the rains, before the blurring mist
disturb the globe of silence where we kissed,
let us be calm and tranquil in its power.

There may be love
as daily and enduring as a glove:
this may be granted when perfection fades,
but never the silken magic that pervades
this first fine tapestry our fingers wove.

Your beauty lifts my heart
to a dimension where time has no part.
It must come down, I know: we take our places
among the normal names and normal faces:
but not in these first hours, not from
the start.

This equilibrium,
most rare and perilous balance, leaves me dumb
to say it all, to name the gems and metals
(flame of a butterfly before it settles)
before the troubles and the questionings come.

Before our ship is tested,
before we sail where seas are cold and crested,
for this one hour let lust be pure as laughter:
let your love breathe without before and after,
soft as the hollow where a bird has rested.

Performers

Tensed, flexing, they make the leap.
Notion to enactment. Flesh gathered to a purpose
 outside its own needs, yet fuelled by them.
Bruised, always ready to be bruised again:
and cherished, suckled, dreaming within a dream
of another dream, never-ending, lit from within
a dream small enough to swallow like a pill,
big enough to wander in hand in hand
with everyone you ever loved, where the present
moment never comes to an end. This is
surely what they are searching for. Look at their eyes.
The dream within the dream: it has to be that.

The trance-state must be catching: normally I
feel my mind realistic, ballasted. Now
among them, I feel less sure. Outlines flicker.
Flat shorelines become thickets of dark-green weed.
A mountain fades into cold white smoke, then becomes
a cloud that hardens into snow. Then thaws.
Let's pretend. And now we've finished pretending,
let's pretend that what we're doing now is real.
And if it isn't real, let's still pretend.
Ought I to resist? They confuse me, but gladly
I embrace confusion.
Their petulant moments,
even, are a sharp game I relish. Why?
What spell do they put on me? It must be the
deep assent they give to transformation.
Their openness is beyond morality.
To take so readily might just as well be to give:

take, give: take, give: the words change places
till one tires of watching: do a swallow's wings
take from the wind, or offer themselves to it?
Their egotism is a sacrifice
of self. I breathe the pyre's sky-dimbing plume.
So the cardboard turns out to be rock, the paints
are really the true colours of nature.
That girl's feigned tears fall for all slow griefs.

To simulate passion is to remember it,
to remember passion is to invite more:
watching them pretend, I become more real:
their rehearsed movements unlock my limbs to freedom.

So ritual makes hard truth into a dream
that could come true. And as Imagination,
the red-nosed clown, squirts from his button-hole,
true laughter rises up, true tears run down.

My Name

(If I lived in a culture whose poets take bardic names,
I would choose to be called Flying-fish.)
Flying-fish loves the salt kiss of brine:
Flying-fish loves the leap into slanting air.

Flying-fish loves the bottle-green of the depths:
his soul expands in the diminishing light.

Flying-fish fears the dry smack of a deck-landing:
Flying-fish fears the ring of grinning captors.

Most of all he abhors the poison-droolers:
the vomit of selfishness, the sea's foul overcoat.

Flying-fish loves the long rhythms of the swell,
he has patience with its settle and swing, settle and swing.

Flying-fish fears the slyness of net and trawl,
he grieves for his brothers who thrash in that stricture.

Flying-fish offers his sperm to the smooth scales of a
mate:
he loves to come close amid the vastness of ocean.

Flying-fish fears the bleep of sonic detectors:
to escape technology, he flashes through air and foam.

Flying-fish is nourished by the marrow of colours,
a rainbow fattens him like a wedding-breakfast.

Flying-fish does not fear death.
Night is friendly to him, and death is night:

calm night on the ocean, with uncountable stars,
and fragrances blowing off the islands.

Flying-fish does not fear death.
But he loves life: he is in no hurry

to resign motion, to float with stiffened fins,
to be part of the sea's phosphorescent detritus.

When the time comes, he will accept night:
meanwhile each morning and evening he splashes and
glides,

in search of more life, singing in water-language:
More, more, more, always let there be more!

'Know Thyself'

A translation into English alliterative metre of the Latin hexameter written by Samuel Johnson on completing his revision of the Dictionary, 1772

Scaliger, when with scant sense of achievement he had scrawled
his lexicon's last page, after prolonged toil, loathing
the mindless menial grind, the small problems piled into
mountains,
in hate groaning, he gave his thought to guide grave judges
that the penal system should prescribe for all hard prisoners
found guilty of devilment, the drudgery of making a dictionary –
one punishment, for the most impenitent, all punishments
compounding!

How right he was, that rare man, erudite, lofty, rigorous,
worthy of weightier work, better able to serve the world
by enchanting the ear with antique heroisms, or the bards'
ecstasies,

the shifting sands of governance, the swirl of the shining spheres
his mind could read and unriddle, and the vast earth's revolving.

A large example is dangerous. The dunciad of learned dolts
glare and grumble, presenting their case, princely Scaliger
as if it were yours, master. Let each mind his measure!
I, at least, have realized that to be your rival (in rage
or in knowledge) was never part of my nature. Who can know
why?
Is it the lazy flow of my chill blood, or the long idle years
that I lost?
Or was I just bundled into the world with a bad brain?
As soon as your sterile work was over, and the stiff
word-stubble

you had pushed through, peerless wisdom the goddess into her
pure
arcanum accepted you, while all the arts applauded,
and the world's words, their voices so long at variance,
now home from exile joyfully rang about you, gentle master,
their joiner.

As for me, my task finished, I find myself still lettered to myself:
the dull doom of doing nothing, harsher than any drudgery,
stays with me, and the staleness of slow stagnation.
Cares beget cares, and a clamouring crowd of troubles
vex me, and vile dreams, the sour sleep of an empty mind.
What will refresh me? The rattle of all-night roisterers,
or the quiet of solitary spaces? Oh, sleep, sleep, I call,
lying where I fret at the lingering night, but fear day's cold
finger.
Trembling, I trudge everywhere, peering, prying, into
everything, trying
passionate to know if somewhere, anyhow, a path leads up to a
more perfect pasture
but glooming over grand schemes I never find my
growing-point,
and am always forced finally to face myself, to own frankly
that my heart is illiterate, and my mind's strength an illusion
I labour to keep alive. Fool, a mind not fuelled by learning
slides into a morass. Stop the supply of marble
to Phidias our fertile sculptor, and where are his forms and
faces?
Every endeavour, every avenue, ends in frustration always,
closed in by lack of cash, bound up by a costive mind.
Ah, when that mind reckons up its resources, the harvest of
reasoning
stacked high, matter for self-satisfaction, is conspicuously absent:
nor does creation's great king from his high castle send down daily
supplies to ensure its survival.

Regularly the years mount up, regularly the mind's works do
not mount up:
as for the frills and the friendly honours, fruits of a useful life,
its own harsh judgement forbids it that harmless enjoyment.
Turning to survey its territory, that night-shadowed tundra,
the mind is full of fear – of ghosts, of the fleeting gleam
of the thin shadows of nothing, the absence of shapes, the
shimmer.

What then am I to do? Let my declining years go down to the
dark?
Or get myself together, gather the last of my gall,
and hurl myself at some task huge enough for a hero?

And if that's too much, perhaps my friends might find me
some dull, decent job, undemanding: like making a
dictionary ...

Blind Man Listening to Radio

I

> Gold and silver carp
> nose to the surface
> of the flat pool. Lily stems
> trail through my fingers.
> The fish have cool, round
> invented voices.

II

> Pacing my dark brown oblong
> I touch the shiny black wood
> of a clarinet. The air
> grows suddenly sweeter.

III

> I nest like a mouse
> in the folds of a great newspaper.
> With a rustle of pages
> I settle my back and shoulders,
> ready for conversation,

IV

> It is morning. The smell of coffee
> and the announcer's calm voice,
> telling of bombs and murder.

V

> A pot of black peat. Seeds
> rain in. Quickly, a flower grows
> Another. Then another.

VI

    A woman's voice
    warmed in a soft throat.

    I think of her rounded body
    tense, on the studio chair.

VIII

    I lie in bed, twirl a serrated knob.
    From my ear, a beam goes out
    across oceans, continents. I taste the crash of surf,
    the wind in the gull's pinions,
    the hard feet of mules in the high passes.

The Seafarer

Translated from the Anglo-Saxon

My purpose is to tell my own true tale,
to find words for my wanderings, how I in work-days
endured harsh times. Bitter troubles
in my heart's hold I have had to bear,
felt care clutch at my keel often.
The waves' chaos has many times caught me
in the ship's prow as she in peril
drove on to rocks. Ravenous cold
grasped my feet, fettered in frost's
cold chains: but the churning cares
were hot to my heart, and inmost hunger
stabbed at my tired mind.

                          Amid soft safety
the man in the land's lap will never learn
how I suffered storm-season and ice-cold sea
far from the soothing of friendly siblings.
Icicles hung from me. Hail came showering,
I heard no sound but the sea's smash,
the freezing swell. Sometimes the swan's voice
gave me a gladness: the gannet's language
or curlew's cry were my only carolling:
I knew no mead-hall, only the mew's call.

On stone cliffs the storms came crashing,
their only answer the icy-feathered
tern's whistle, and the wild shriek
of the horn-beaked eagle. No kin of my hearth
was near to comfort my needy spirit.

Ah, little he knows, who has lived
safe from such hell-journeys, in land's shelter
pouring wine, proud, how on sea-paths
I, wary, have watched and waited.
Night came down in darkness, north-snow driving,
frost gripped the earth, hail hit the ground
hardest of corn. Yet my heart cries out,
my heart that rules me, that the rearing waves,
salt water's tumult, I should try for myself.
Without cease my spirit spurs me:
hunger of mind keeps me homeless,
seeking far places and foreign people.

Yet there is none above ground so great-hearted,
so ready with gifts, so reckless with youth,
so lion-brave, by his lord so loved,
as so tempt the sea-tracks and never tremble
at what harms the Most High may have waiting.
That man has no mind for fine rings or harp-music,
worldy wishes, or the joy of women:
his thought is of naught but the wave's thrashing.

The woods are in blossom, towns grow brighter,
the fields fairer, earth's pulse faster,
and it all serves only to stir the striving
mind to movement, in him who mean
to venture far across the flood-ways.
Likewise the cuckoo, with unlucky voice,
welcomes summer but warns of sorrow
bitter in breast's hold.

                    Blissful he knows not,
the secure man, what some mus suffer
on homeless roads who roam the farthest.
Even now my soul strays from my breast's stowage,
my spirit flies over the flood-fields,
wide-wandering in the whale's kingdom,

in earth's far reaches – then to me returns
greedy and hankering. The helpless heart
is called by the winging bird to the whale's way,
the immense waters. But the Almighty's
delights draw me more than this death-in-life,
brief loan of breath. I have no belief
that the good things of earth can be eternal.
Three things threaten every man's thoughts,
keep him in doubt till his doom's day:
illness, age or the sword's edge:
for every wayfarer, one of them waits.
For that reason, the rightest repute
for any hero, the highest hearsay,
is the love of the living. Before he leaves
this earth, he should earn, in spite of enemies,
the fair fame of fighting the devil,
that the sons of men should commend him
and his bright blazon be among the blessed
for a life without limit, eternity's largeness,
great among the graced.

                    Days grow shorter,
earth's pride palls, lordship is poorer.
No kings come now, nor conquering Caesars,
no gold-givers like those who are gone:
those amongst whom were the mightiest marvels
famed in their time as a fearless fellowship.
Those dauntless are departed, their glory dimmed:
weaker men walk the earth now, and wield power:
their having is a heaviness.

                    Fame is hushed,
the world's dignity withers up and shrivels
as comes to every man now over middle-earth:
age presses on him, his face grows pale,
white-haired, he sorrows for his henchmen,
sons of greatness given to the ground.

His garment of flesh, as life goes from it,
loses sweetness, relish and suffering-shock,
neither his hand nor his brain can hold a burden.
And though for his born brother he will bury
treasure in the tomb, strew the grave with gold,
various riches, to rig fair his voyage,
yet if the departed soul was sin-darkened
no gold will keep off the grimness of God,
though he had deftly deceived those he dwelt among.

Great is the Maker's awe, it moves the earth,
which He fastened on a firm anchorage:
the reaches of land and the sky's rim.
A fool has no God-fear; unready death finds him,
but heaven's grace homes in to the humble-hearted:
the Faether fixes such minds on a foundation of faith.
A man must rule himself with a strong heart, and steadily,
his word be trusted, his ways clean,
Every man must have dealings meetly
with friend and with foe…disaster*…
and the friend he has found shall in the flames
of a pyre be powdered: Fate is more powerful,
the All-Mover mightier than a man's wishes!

Now let our hearts think where is their true home
and take counsel how we can come there,
and labour also that we may be allowed
to be in the abode of blessedness,
the right place for life, in God's love's realm,
and heaven's hopes.

        Now thank we the Holy One
that he, the world's Prince, put a price on us:
for all time, the Lord eternal.

                                AMEN.

The manuscript is defective at this point.

From *Open Country (1986)*

George Orwell, in Barcelona, Imagines Jura

Cold air from the mountains.
This thin tunic was someone else's. I should
have got kitted out properly: a British Warm
(going cheap any time since I was fifteen,
good Cotswold wool, none of this Southern trash,
discipline stitched into every seam:
something left to us by those straight-backed men
who disappeared into the mud): I might have felt
as if I were on active service then,
not playing soldiers with this bunch of clowns
half comic, half pathetic. Brave though, brave.
Shall I be brave like them, when the clear air
sings loud with bullets? when the cold peaks look down
on bodies sprawled as I remember them
in the *Illustrated London News* when I was twelve,
belly down on the carpet before the fire,
chin on my elbows, turning the shiny pages,
aghast at finding what grown men had to do.

A time of beginnings. Hope blowing in the air,
Hope for what? To be done, I suppose, with greed:
greed that can afford to buy death and wounds:
greed rich enough to collect the toys of power –
steel gratings, sound-proof cells, and men
who feel secure in uniform.

Sometimes, in the night, I feel we might as well
try to break down the mountains that stand
round or empty out the sea.

Yet, after all,
there was a time before the mountains were:
and even the sea is just a bowl of salt.

We have to press on. They attack. We attack. There is
no stopping. It is a set of iron wheels
that cannot stop till something is chewed up.
Who will be chewed to nothing? We or they?
No one knows yet. It will be decided.
That is what we are here for, to decide it.

These chopped-straw cigarettes make me cough. But the air,
in its coldness, floods my chest like hope.
The incitement of melting snow: a time
of beginnings. What did the blind man write?
'Or breath of vernall air from snowie Alpe.'
The scattered detritus of that education
they worked so long to give me.

One day, one day, I will go back to it.

One day, if our side wins. One day, if this
iron time ever passes, when the puppets
can put on the mobile faces of men and women
and the soft, rounded, growing limbs of children:
when greed and war are beaten to a standstill
or pursued with demons to some other planet
to hatch their empires there: one day, I shall
be at peace under a roof of sloping stones,
with fowl pecking outside, and the sea's voice:
a different sea from the hard dark line out there
that slices at the sky with its cutting edge:
a sea with tides, and rock-basins, and seals.
And then I shall mix myself a fuller palette
beyond these blacks and whites and greys, if that
day comes.
Yes, then I shall go back.
to a life more simple than this of war, and more complex.

All my books so far have been calls to action.
In that stone house with a stack of turf outside
I shall build some shelves, and on the highest one,
almost out of reach even for me,
I shall store my call-to-action books. Not so
as to disown them, just to say *Their war
is over. Stand at ease, good soldier
whose long day's fighting has earned a quiet shelf.*

The firelight will play on their faded jackets,
and I shall turn to a stack of new white sheets.
No more clarion-calls. The work I shall be about
will have the calm of a boulder on the shore,
the colour and fragrance of the hillside gorse
and its perceptions will be sharp as peat-smoke.
These fine shades incite to action, of a kind.

Or to the slow maturing of attitudes:
the subsoil, the peat, from which action will form itself..
the long slow maturation, the root-fibres.

But nothing realised in one generation.

But the colours of intimidation are primary.
Threatened people must act before nightfall.
What drove me always to herd with the threatened?
Whatever that force was, I welcome it.
I welcome kinship with the gaunt and ragged.
I eat the proffered crust. They can have
my carcase if it will be of any use.

But the nuances? The shifting colours?
We all have them, even these people have them,
in the hours when they rest and listen to the grasshoppers:
if those hours came to them more often
I could rest too, I could hear the grasshoppers.
And then the characters I draw in outline
could be filled in. Spirit, breath, and being.

I know what they say about me. I make puppets,
and art is about people.

                    But puppets act,
they jerk their limbs and throw themselves about,
dance, perform tasks, then knock each other flat.
They act when someone pulls their strings. Who pulls?
Over there, among the mountain peaks,
the Fascists pull. Down here, we pull:
the ones who keep alive some dream of kindliness.
Oh, I could give my life to chiaroscuro,
and the rainbow-trout colours of sensibility
and I could do it with a clear conscience
because there is a fullness of truth in it.
Wholeness of life is complex:
when I tell my puppet stories I am simplifying.
But life itself, in our time, simplifies.
Hunger, imprisonment, beatings are simplicities.
The thugs have robbed the people. And one of the things
they have robbed them of is their complexity.

Those English writers contemplating choices!
Virginia wondering who will go to the lighthouse
and for what finely balanced reasons... I respect her,
as I respect a painter who gives years
to catching the swirl of a stream beneath a bridge,
or the slant of light on a London chimney-pot.

I am with the people who are robbed,
forced to live the simplicities of animals.
One day, both they and I will shed that starkness,
if our side wins. I shall have a stone house,
whitewashed, and coloured fowl pecking outside.
There will be no disdainful Pyrenees,
just stony, rounded hills, the home of curlews.
The sea will talk to itself, and I shall listen.

The fowl will cluck, and drawl. I shall sit watching
the sky change colour as the clouds move over.

George Orwell, in Jura, Imagines Barcelona

It seems so long since I saw a lizard.
These rocks have never been hot:
not since the first volcano.

Strange that Eileen should have died first.
There are no simplicities among these mists.
This is Fingal's country.

Sitting at tables in the Ramblas: small, bitter cups of black coffee
Eileen would remember that.

Small, bitter cups also of betrayal.
Hot sunlight defining each tile
on the roof of the telephone exchange.

The Ramblas between us and the Guardia Civil.
Roof-top to roof-top.
We agreed not to fire.

Behind them was the coiled spring of Hitler.
Four years later London was burning.
Bricks too hot for a lizard.

Paving-stones too hot for a scorpion:
and I saw the dead people again,
as in the *Illustrated London News*.

Strange that Eileen should have died first.
The Fascists were trying to get me.
They got her.

She died in their fascist war.
Bombs, fatigue, not enough to eat:
she grew white and weary.

Strange that Eileen should have died first.
She loved me in the days of simplicities.
She sent cigars to the Lenin barracks.

In that hard vertical light
simplicities grew: ideals, a shared smoke,
a bullet through the neck.

Now, here, the light is evanescent
as even Virginia could have wished,
(and she is dead too).

This is Fingal's country.
In these mists that coil and thin
I could believe in sea-serpents.

Last nightfall, looking from the headland
to where the spray mates with the mist
in the shimmer of the sunset colours,

a dark hump seemed about to surface.
Was it only a rock below the tide?
I expected a talking whale.

There are no seals in the Mediterranean;
lizards lie on the hot rocks.
Legends of mermaids are Atlantic.

The big grey father seals
look dog-like in the water,
but turn their heads and stare like men.
I think of the surf-haunting dugong,
a ton of clumsy mammal
wallowing in collapsing waves.

In Barcelona, I was a dugong.
I wallowed along the Ramblas
while the quick lizards peered out.

I was a talking whale
haloed in my own mist and spray.
Now I, too, am dying.

Sea-Lanes

Birthday Poem for Charles Causley

All those small harbours, fretted from the rock
of our dour coastline by the slurping sea,
we know them in brown-shadowed photographs
as they were then:

when did they change so totally? Strange, now,
that windows, walls and roofs we are looking at
are still there just as the antique lens held them:
the harbour office,

the tiered cottages, the steeple on the hill,
these still remain: but what of the human tide,
heavy with pods and salt, that washed about them?
Hardly a sailor

comes to these places now. The tides are there,
the jetty, clock, and lighthouse, but the ships
have gone to the breaker's yard. Ranged, confident,
in the sepia weather

we can still study that tangle of masts and spars,
and as the decades pass, the churning steamers,
smoke-stacks trained on the sky. Round them, oared craft
jostle like minnows:

and if by staring at it with sufficient
intensity, we could will ourselves back into
one of those scenes aglow with Victoria's sunset,
we'd find the fish-scaled

streets that climb from water-line to sky
echoing with sailors' voices, deep-sea talk:

the blue reek of their twist clouding pub windows,
and off the Horn

or in the fog and icebergs of St John's
or swaying clutched in the Sargasso weed,
old men with fine-meshed wrinkles edging their eyes
from scanning distances

would live it all again. For the last time,
as it turned out: their tribe became extinct
in less than half a lifetime. Why? The usual
reason: Technology,

dragging its heavy chain of money, crawled
resistless and unresting over their charts,
their memoried skill, their clustered masts, their talk.
The banker followed

where the inventor led, as he always does:
small ships are uneconomic: only the monsters,
carrying grotesque amounts, using a few
deep-water ports,

computerized neo-Swiftian floating islands,
ugly, forbidding, remote, outward expressions
of greed and the anxiety that nurtures greed,
stolidly pounding

across the oceans of the world, till something
goes wrong and they break in half (a heavy sea
finding the weakness in that stretched-out spine)
and sailors drown,
and the black oil pours out to sink the birds
and suffocate the seals, and the insurers
pay up, and another cliff-tall hull is launched.
The grove of masts
that grew in the green water of the harbours went down
under the axe of Money/Progress:

the sailors, beached, were dwindled into folk-lore,
like Captain Cat,

then vanished. (The folk-lore stage might have been spared.)
Now if Money and Progress were all that mattered,
as city board-rooms think it is, that would
have been the end.

The shallow ports, the simple sheltered inlets,
had seen their centuries of usefulness out.
Their reaches could be left to elvers and herons,
and kids with jam-jars.

In fact that didn't happen. Like a well
with buckets, one trade emptied, another filled.
The piles of slates and mounds of china clay,
the waiting carts,
these went, and with them went the wind-dried men
whose memories held the Horn, the snow, the icebergs,
the salt-caked clothes, the rats and cockroaches,
and as they ebbed

the new tide swirled in Dormobiles and trailers
to the trim week-end hulls. Bank managers
discussed tide-tables with psychiatrists.
Absurd? Of course,

but Charles, we recognize the hunger there,
the need for that ancient wrestle with the sea.
Man seeks a humanly intelligible danger:
something to test

his fibre against. His economic life
is trapped in a dead cocoon of filing-cards,

computers, plastics. Nothing in his survival
dictates that he,

127

his siblings or descendants, should ever go
anywhere near the sea; the populace, indeed,
who take their trips abroad from inland airports,
have, for the most part,

never been on a ship. But memory lives
more strongly in bone-marrow than in the cells
of the wakeful brain. In all the coastal peoples
of Western Europe

a man or a woman here and there goes back
to the tides, the cliffs, the swell, where life depends
on staying awake enough to read a compass.
Often, in fog,

the looming tankers run them down: in storm,
waves rip out their aluminium masts. Where once
men stood and looked at the mocking waves and thought,
Face them, or starve, now starving has nothing to do with sailing,
they come
to challenge the sea again, to dip and scurry,

and even dare the Atlantic in craft as frail
as bicycles,

and though they look funny, Charles, with their yellow
gum-boots and little vanities, you and I find them
worth saluting as, dodging assorted monsters,
they ride the sea-lanes.

Prospero's Staff in the Earth

I'll break my staff,
Bury it certain fathoms in the earth,
And deeper than did ever plummet sound
I'll drown my book.

The drowned book, yes;
I see it sifting down:
the paper bunching like seaweed
then riffling, opening,
showing its pages in the subacqueous light,
showing its symbols to the staring cod
and the expressionless lobster:
the stitched spine holding,
the ink not fading because it was magic ink,
the round o's of the figures like eyes
staring up at the feet of sea-birds,
floating and swaying between sea and sky:
and in the end shredding out,
dwindling to wisps of pulp,
the stored thoughts veining into ocean-streams,
brooks of knowledge in the thick salt gloom,
defined channels of wisdom, but not permanent,
dispersed, dispersed, and in the end forgotten:
all this I can see.

But the staff in the earth!
'Certain fathoms' suggests meditation,
suggests calculation, an arrived-at point
below the pathways of mole and beetle,
below the drinking-threads of casual shrubs,
its grave neighbours the roots of the strong trees,

just above the level of the hardest rocks:
just above our planet's carapace.

Were the grains astonished?
In the silence that came down after the magician,
up there in the evening light, had walked away,
having murmured the last incantations,
the valedictions:
when tall Prospero, without staff or book,
turned his face naked to the sunset's fire,
and the grains that held the newcomer
were left to their long vigil.
These grains also had their dignity, their stored
and memoried selves were of many noble kinds;
there was the self of milled rock, and of humus,
end of the seasonal mould of leaves:
end of the long-dispersed flesh of animals
and birds: and their bones, which were not dispersed,
but lay quietly in their original diagrams,
the structure of their first agile inheritors:
almost as quietly as the stones, with their calm
vocabulary of stillness.
Did the stranger
startle or challenge the bones and grains?

Everything about it was strange.
What was the bark? What was the grained wood?
What tree nourished it, and when
let it fall?

Surely that was an unknown tree.
What soil held its roots? Not the soil
of this place, or any place
visited by sailors.

Was it single, the only tree of its kind.
or were there six in a ring

in some secret place of the world?
What jewelled birds perched there,
or were they dark, hooded birds?
Was there transformation?
Did the staff change slowly into something else?
And as it changed, did it impart its knowledge
a throb at a time to the hard roots about it,
till one by one its atoms fell away:
till in the end there was only the memory
that a core of secrets once lay in the earth
in a spot that was marked with no memorial,
only a patch of soil like any other?
And, up in the light and air, a grove of trees
alive with birds, the ordinary common birds?

Perhaps it happened that way. Perhaps not.
And perhaps that was not the most important thing.

The most important thing was the forgiveness.

The staff was buried because the quarrel was.

The magic died with no one left to hate.

It was the cheated man who studied runes:
on the atoll of his rejection he brooded over spells
that pulled into the drag of vengeance-
tides the usurer's hull, his masts, his decks, his people.

The quiet grass grows over battlefields:
gentle slopes we walk on, cow-pastures
soaked up hot blood once, rang with hideous yells
of agony or equally hideous joy.

The peaceful grass grows on. This is the miracle.
Where Cain struck Abel down, the daisy's eye
opens each dawn in accustomed innocence.
So on the island of Prospero's rough magic
the polished staff put knowledge in the earth,

the highest knowledge and yet the commonest, fragrant
as breath of cows, majestic as the clouds.

While off the rocky point, the book sways down
to the sea-bed, and the magician's house
feels once again the pulse of life, the warmth,
the healing flesh, the young man and the girl.

Twofold

A Sequence of Fourteen Poems

1

Celebrating
a symbiosis:
taking note of a successful
graft or splice or inlay or dovetail
of the one nervous system with the other,
bringing unison, bringing two-moving-as-one:

and marvelling at

two spines, one vertical, one horizontal,
two brains, one carried low for finding out,
one carried aloft six feet above the stones:

thinking of the delicate
communication, the wordless talking,
the sharing of perception and impulse, the trusting,
the identification, the mutuality so endless
so difficult to pin down with a neat description
we might as well give up and call it love:

thinking of these things,
marvelling,
celebrating these things,
I will sing, I will sing.

2

They shape a moving geometry
a not-quite-fearful symmetry

his spine straight and tall
is the triangle's back wall

133

the taut leash the hypotenuse
her supple pads guiding his patient shoes

dictate the amalgam's progression
in calm Euclidean fashion

and as Euclid pondered
on forms that never wandered

beyond the reach of laws
hedged in like grazing cows

in necessity's green pastures
holding their logical postures

so thought with its true hold
plots the moves of Twofold

where impulses cluster
cool brain must be master

but the spirit's deep wells
nourish the brain-cells.

3

A duet of species finely performed, and also
an equally fine duet of genders, as I

imagine Twofold. Not, of course, inevitable:
some blind men must be led by male dogs, some blind

women by female dogs, some by male: still, most
guide-dogs are bitches, and in my mind's eye

for no better reason than being male myself
I see the upright partner as a man.

I see the female perception guiding the male
investigating, reacting, preparing the ground

for the steps he makes towards a planned destination.
I see the female in light, the male in darkness.

She is familiar with contour and contingency,
with events' texture, with corners' abruptness:

he builds in darkness a world of intentions:
landscapes blossom within that globe of shadow.

He wants to construct the world according to his needs:
she needs to want the world in order to construct.

His is the strength, the onward-driving passion,
hers is the guiding and sustaining element:

as some great whale migrating across the world
follows the path of a stream within the ocean.

4

I was little. Dam, warm coat,
smell of good, Smooth, naked dugs.
Tug, drink. Other me's, push
for a dug. Then roll. Paws.
Straw. Was there straw?

Standups took me to a strange place.
No straw. Boards. In the big air,

hardness: rough pads. Pavement,
they kept saying, Pavement.
Where did they go, the other me's?
Did dam stay there?
Is her coat still warm,
somewhere?
Does good smell the same?

I have a warm coat. But no
small me's. Standups gave me a sleep,
I woke up sick. After that,
dogs did not smell good:
dugs are somewhere else.
Pavement, pavement is my world.

5

I know smell-talk. A smell means *come, sniff.*
Turn here. Stop. Sniff.

Stand-ups told me No.
No smell.
Go forward. Dog-smell, man-smell,
sharp hunting cat-rabbit smell,
dustbin come-and-search smell,
earth-after-rain smell, saying *Dig,*
scratch: all No.

Go forward.
He has to go forward.
Standups do not know smell. It is not
their way of talking.
They use ears, eyes.
His ears. My eyes.
Go forward.

6

Safe: raised up
on a small cliff, steep quick sides
but short, easy. Yes, but big
in feeling. Down, trouble.
Danger. Fear. Could be the end
of light, warm. Could be crushed
broken bones, hurt. Up, good.

Up on the small cliff, feet-scuff.
Standups walking, slow, quick.
Trousers. Skirts with sway.
Skirts with no sway. Boots.
All move, a river of Standups,
to where the small cliff stops.
Now: Watch. Listen. Eyes up
for lights. Or a green Standup
walking in a round eye.

Mostly, no lights. Just look
for Rollers being still. They
are waiting to kill us.
Make them wait.
When Standups walk, walk.
To the next cliff. Slow
as you go up: his foot
feels for safe. Safe comes.

7

Till I was seven, I had sight.
Light and dark built alternate worlds
One, two, day, night, time's footfalls.
I know what a house looks like,
a tree, a hedge; table, chair,
man, woman. I know clouds.
I know what a dog looks like.
I know what my dog looks like.

She sees me. I do not see her.
She sees house, table, chair, tree,
hedge. She knows the closed eye of night,
the open of day.
But drably.
Her vision is monochrome, or nearly so.
I remember more sight than she sees.

I can recall the colour of butter,
eggs, bread, oranges. I can say *Red*
and watch red grow in the blackness,
flow, bloom, spread, fire to warm the world.
Yellow is a dancing daffodil trumpet.
Green is lying down in coolness. Blue, ah,
blue is my secret festival. When I
was five, I dipped a white stick in a tin
of blue paint, on our garage floor.
I took it out. It dripped and trailed: Blue,
it said, Blue, Joy in blue. Joy in blue.

8

She is programmed for work.
He is programmed for leisure, friends, talk, music
and work.

Her work is to walk Twofold.
His is the Law. In a house
with others, he sits in quiet
rooms. Trees swish outside. He has
the quietest office, at the back.

All the others have eyes. He, sound-bound
has the most need of quiet. His ears
need to be focussed, fenced from disturbance.

Tree-swish and (muffled beyond doors) keyboard-tap.

Sometimes, her sigh. Stretched out
beneath the desk, her warm flank close
to his still feet.
Work, work.

9

We journey to the big talk-kennel.
Hello-voices. Coffee-smell. Then the long
waiting, under the wood he rests his hands on.
Standups come in. He says, *Sit*.
He voices them. They voice him.
Often they use their sounds that are like ours,
their that-hurts whine, their let-me-outwhine,
their alarm bark.

He voices on, always the same.
Easy, easy, quieting them.
They touch hands. They go.
More come.

10

They come to me to hear the law, to know
if the law will give them a little scope to live,
get someone off their back, even things out.

They have eyes, usually two per person, that drink
in the blessing of colour, the joy of light,
but colour and light are blurred by a crust of sorrow

Their eyes serve as the gathering-point of tears
and when they look, it is with greed and fear
at what another has.
For my own part,

I do not seem to have much greed and fear.
My sorrow is channelled into one deep well.
I have not many grudges to avenge.

At my approach, people become more gentle.
They put away the clubs and the long knives
they use on one another: as if they thought
to be blinded is already club and knife,
enough to bear.

And so they sit and weep,
and stutter out the tale of loss and outrage
that brings them to my door. And I sit
here, calm, taking notes with subtle finger-tips,

Who knows injustice better than I? Knows better
simply what happens is the force that rules?
Yet I explain the law, the law, the law.

11

August. A velvet night.
They tell me the moon is full.
I lie awake, throw back the covers, feel
on my skin the cleanness of the air.
That means the world outside
is flooded with the moon's calm light.

I feel the clarity:
I listen to the light. A bell-tower
chimes over there, beyond the orchard.

Waves of bell-sound come to me over sleeping
apple-boughs. I hear her twitch an ear:
it almost wakes her, almost communicates
some message: but what could it be?

Does she know what a bell is?
Does she know what apples are?
Not as I know them: yet they say
wild dogs, and even some that live in kennels,
howl when the moon is full.

12

Evening. It is feeding-time for both.
Others will set food before him, but first
he feeds her.

The tin, in its expected place.
Round, smooth, heavy. One knowing hand,
the left, holds it table-steady: the right
drives in the harsh diminutive
sword-point of the tin-opener. Press, turn:
press, tum: a jagged circle falls
clean out. Repeat other end. Now push
a cylinder of meat and sliding fat
into her waiting dish.

Now crush in biscuits, scraps. A swill of milk.
He feels her waiting, hears her looking up.

So: place the dish. Then soap and towel.
Clean hands. Now it is his turn to be fed.

But as she licks and swallows, he is aware
she nourishes for him. Nerve-impulses,
blood-density, soft marrow and hard bone,
satellite brain. Her pads are his fore-toes.
Her rough pelt sprouts from his scalp. Her eyes
are his two eyes, on snail-stalks.

The tin of meat he neatly circles out
feeds him. He murmurs grace.

13

They call the day over, lie down in attitudes
of relinquishment. Sleep folds in both spheres.

Singly, they lie, each exploring the individual
labyrinth of unconsciousness,
wired to contrasting
diagrams. She patrols a thicket of residual
day-actions, brittle as firewood. His more lasting
sleep-catacombs, fanged with memory's stalactites,
invite sober pacing, abound in rounded opaque
metaphor. Nothing connects their two nights
except the slumber that rounds them like a coiled snake,

unhitching their duality, refreshing them with a respite
of singleness. When light wakes them,
all the more willingly they build themselves back into Twofold:
connect, gear in, dance to their unheard music.

14

As grateful as the hand that warms the glove
their pliancy of trust. Has it a name?
We might as well give up and call it love.

This mutuality I'm thinking of
as double as two windows in one frame
is grateful as the hand that warms the glove.

Such woven trust of two, what does it prove?
Is it a dance, a combat or a game?
We might as well give up and call it love.

What eye can count the wing-beats of a dove?
Their rapid impulse-sharing is the same,
as grateful as the hand that warms the glove.

Gentle as leaves that whisper in a grove,
sudden as sparks that whirl above a flame:
we might as well give up and call it love.

Though strict neurology may disapprove,
I had to use the only words that came:
as grateful as the hand that warms the glove.
We might as well give up and call it love.

Mid-Week Period Return

Home Thoughts of a Native

This poem was commissioned by Mr Roger Pringle, whose Celandine Press in Stratford-upon-Avon was bringing out a volume of verse tributes to John Betjeman. I had published a severe review of Summoned by Bells about twenty years earlier and had ever since seen myself mentioned among Betjeman's 'attackers,' 'decriers,' etc., whereas in fact I had come through the years to have a much higher opinion of his poetry; so I threw myself into the writing of a poem for him, in topographical vein, with such enthusiasm that the result, as Mr Pringle pointed out when he received it, was amusingly too long. If he had printed it there would have been no room in the book for anything else. He solved the problem by printing a short extract in the commissioned volume and bringing out the complete text, with drawings by Arthur Keene, in 1982.

I took the railway from Oxford to Stoke-on-Trent
and JB was with me every mile I went.

These are the two towns that mean most to me
where I have lived longest and feel most free

from the cramps and constrictions of this our dour epoch
since each in its own way has managed to stop the clock

enough to celebrate in sharply contrasting scenes
some rearguard victory of the men over the machines:

and I looked out of the window as the train clattered along
and felt JB's presence always persistent and strong

for he loves England and holds her in his heart
though like me he has had to watch her body torn apart

and her spirit travestied and misunderstood
in our age of lasting evil and evanescent good.

In fact I think of Betjeman very often:
his deftly-drawn images have refused to fade or soften

and some of them have been with us for fifty years.
There is an instinctive truth in the course he steers.

I have found things in his work to praise and blame:
most literate people could probably say the same.

But he speaks to me always of England, her follies and bounties.
He is a presence in London, in the Home Counties,

in Pembrokeshire or Lincoln or on the Berkshire downs,
but most of all in Oxford, ravaged queen of towns,

where he went to school and felt young life unfolding,
not yet foreseeing the nightmares of William Golding.

He knows his Oxford, his young eyes were among the last
to see her stately with the beauty that changed to past

on the day Morris opened his factory in Cowley:
William Morris! Irony of his being so named, who foully

shattered the centuries-old balance of Tillage and Thought
by throwing across it a new city that could never be taught

the secrets of either, the incurable infection
of a clumsy transplant resulting in tissue rejection.

I have never hated Morris, nor felt unforgiving
about a man who simply wanted a living

for himself and others, to keep the job-wires humming:
still, anyone with normal vision could have seen it coming,

and it would not have hurt Morris to have been persuaded
to build up his industry where it could have been aided

by an existing work-force and industrial tradition,
instead of committing moral and aesthetic sedition,

however unconsciously, by letting his monster loose
to wring the neck of Oxford like a Christrnas goose

waddling on Port Meadow all the years I remember
then suddenly disappearing about mid-December

to hang in the poulterers' shops as Oxford hangs now.
These thoughts weigh on me as the train pulls past the Plough

Inn at Wolvercote where I drink, and past my own
house, a scribbled-over-with-green box of stone,

and as the train gathers speed and leaves Oxford behind
they hang like chill stalactites from the roof of my mind..

On my journey I paid little attention to churches
and none to suburbs with paving and silver birches

but I always had a loving eye for canals and rivers
which are arteries and boundaries and importance-givers.

In the Cherwell Valley there are two water-courses
each with its own way of obeying nature's forces.

The canal lies in a series of rational grand curves
following the land's contours. With delighted dashes and swerve

the river offers a sweet wilful parody of that logic,
making its rationality seem bland and pedagogic,

now coming so close as to share the same fringe of reeds,
now withdrawing in pursuit of its own secret needs.

Rejoice in it, rejoice while it is still to be seen,
while the soft grey sky brings out the richness of the green,

for the men who want to make all England a speedway for heavy
trucks
are planning to murder the grass and the willows, the reeds and the
swimming ducks,

and when the bulldozers come the Cherwell Valley will go:
and the fouled river struggling on somewhere below

and the choked canal canopied in noise and fumes
will have died for our England that consumes, consumes, consumes.

The train rattles and sways, then the train slows,
to halt at another place this poet knows.

Leamington. The metal python-loops of the bridge
slide by. Below, a glimpse of the street, and shops.
There used to be a bookshop there, where I once

bought a set of Dickens (Chapman and Hall) and a book
that had belonged to Philip Larkin (*Characters of the Seventeenth
Century*, ed. Nichol Smith, Oxford, 1920; why

did he sell it?). The young JB used to take
the train here from Oxford for the afternoon,
walk about and look at the buildings: wrote

one of his best poems about it, 'Death
in Leamington'. With a more urgent tremor I recall
this is where the train from Stratford starts and ends.

It loiters from station to station, names like Bearley
and Wilmcote, fields and lanes and hillsides
I have seen many times, but always in summer,

so that to me it is the English summer train,
cottage gardens with loaded fruit-trees, roadside grass
standing tall and feathery, with dandelions and rust-red

sorrel heads. And then Stratford!, wide open
of course to the tourist industries of the world, but still
with the flavour of a market town, and really an unusual

number of Tudor buildings, not all on show
with clicking turnstiles. Some people, nose in air, have
'no patience with Stratford'. I have no patience with

people who have no patience with Stratford, partly
because it was the magic place of my youth,
where with young friends I wandered on summer evenings

or in dew-fresh mornings before the coaches came,
and partly because in that big red-brick barn
they act out his stories, his singing parables.

Through the stretched-out years, on pin-pointed evenings,
hat and coat folded under the seat, souvenir programme
in hand, I have sat with switched-on eyes and ears:

taking in the nightingale grief of Juliet,
the tall dignity of Othello's pain,
or Shylock with his rigid Old Testament soul

seeing revenge and law and a daughter's obedience
in the stark primary colours of the Middle East:
and Autolycus has sung and Falstaff laughed and groaned.

The train rattles and sways, then the train slows,
to halt at another place this poet knows.

Nobody praises Birmingham. At least
if praise exists, I haven't come across it.
And yet the place rouses in me no real
hostility, no scorn or deep revulsion:
nothing to prompt me to a satire like
'Come, friendly bombs, and fall on Slough'(how well
I can recall the shiver of fierce joy
which seized me when I came across that line
while still at school, the comradeship of knowing
that someone else hated the things I hated).

No, I could never write a 'Slough' about
flaccid old Brum, nor, I suspect, could he.
A lot of honest work has gone on there,
mostly in metal, and there have been artists:

Burne-Jones and William Morris (the real one),
and John Henry Newman, and behind them
the young Sam Johnson finding himself a wife.

And in our time, the University:
A. M. D. Hughes discoursing on Literature
(a man of the rarest cultivation of mind)
and the young Helen Gardner in his department,
and teaching classics, the young Louis MacNeice
(patient of 'Homer in a Dudley accent'), and Auden
growing up just outside, at Solihull.
The light has never gone completely out.
No, Birmingham is not quite Slough or Uxbridge.

Clearer than Scafell Pike, my heart has stamped on
The view from Birmingham to Wolverhampton.

So wrote the Auden of the youthful English mind
before he left our way of thinking behind

and moved to where the people were strangers and the open spaces
really were open, where the dour vigilant faces

of his own tribe were no longer there to accuse him
though in their devoted hunger to exploit and use him

his new hosts proved even more expert at removing his scalp
till he had to hide away on top of an Austrian alp

where people would leave him alone to get his breath,
and finally came back to Oxford to wait for death.

Well, it is over now, and as the train pulls past
blank windows and canal sluices I can reconcile at last

the minor Atlantic Goethe whose hobby was theology
and the schoolboy so bright-eyed about mining and geology.

Now the menhirs of industrial pre-history slide by,
the eighteenth century crumbles under a Diesel-thick sky:

This part of Birmingham is called Soho, a better spectacle
even in its ruin than London's brim-full receptacle

of all the detritus of flaked skin, toenails and vomit
left when millions share a cold sexual dream and from it

never quite manage to wake. The acres of wrecked cars
rusting in the Midland rain are at least better than the bars

full of pimps and transvestites and lonely ostriches
with heads in the muddy sand between neon-lit ditches.

About mid-point one seems to sense a thinning
of the rails and sheds and tips, almost the beginning

of a trampled mud-patch of country, here a strip of grazing
for a horse, there a chicken run, but so far from phasing

down, the industrial tangle resumes at once: Wolverhampton
is part of the tarnished breastplate Birmingham has clamped on.

The train rattles and sways, then the train slows,
and now we have left the England this poet knows,

because from Wolverhampton we move through Stafford to Stoke
where JB's Victorian connoisseurship seems a joke

in another language, and his Anglican piety
a conjuring trick in the old twice -nightly variety.

Yet his or not, it is England, and he must
be aware what good things lie beneath clay-slip and coal-dust.

> My city was built for a wedding,
> nave, aisle and altar:
> the bride and the bridegroom are treading
> a dance without falter.

> He shines black, she pale as a moon:
> she is kneaded, he broken.
> But their strength is united, and soon
> the blessing is spoken.

149

The coal fires the clay, the clay
shines back to the coal:
and the man in his brief passing day
adds his touch to the whole.

This marriage is important and also complex and strange:
between them the parties cover almost the whole range

of forms of being. He began as vegetation,
trunks, bark, leaves, roots: untold aeons of gestation

and millions of tons of rock-pressure were needed
to evolve his glossed brittleness and stored warmth. She proceeded

by an even more surprising route: basically stone
milled by incalculable time to a paste, but also bone,

the skulls, limbs and rib-cages of vegetarian beasts,
powdered and mixed in till translucency increased

and with it tensile strength, the resistance to impact.
So the groan-haunted slaughterhouse plays its part, and in fact

both coal-mine and pot-bank are slaughterhouses too:
miners are trapped and entombed, and of potters a few

have always let in death through their mouths and noses:
my father's father died of potter's silicosis.

And now I get out and stand beside the train
happy to see that steeple-crowned hill again,

the tall church in whose shadow I learnt to read
the miraculous black marks that answered my deepest need.

In the moving crowd I stand, a silent, grateful man,
since this place, for me, is where it all began.

Here, coal and clay come together to breed a city
where life is strong and resilient though never pretty,

and this city is where the story began for me,
and still goes on. This poem is for JB.

The Shipwreck

For a Painting by J. M. W. Turner

This canvas yells the fury of the sea.
Across a quiet room, where people murmur
their poised appreciations, it shrieks out
the madness of the wind.
How can that be?
Woven of voiceless threads, its pigments laid
with'no more sound than the mice make', it hurls
the tempest at my eardrums, and my eyes
smart in the lashing spray. But not before
the colours of tragedy have enkindled them:
it must be so, because the colours hold
the secret. They are noise, and tilt, and steepness.
The colours are trough, and crash, the cry of gulls
lifted and blown away like part of the spume.
The colours are the bawling of the wind.
That yellow sail, its mast snapped sideways, catches
into itself and holds that gleam of light
amid the livid waters, the evening gleam
through torn black cloud as the sullen day departs.
One last message of life. Over and out.
The people in the small escaping boat
(too frail for the uncaring slide and smash
of those tall water-cliffs, promising only
ten minutes more of life, of clinging on
before the toppling plunge) see in that yellow
the last of life that they will ever see.

A goodbye signal, perhaps a welcoming
to those new neighbours, whoever they will be,
who wait for them on the other side of darkness,
below the clap of the waves and lace of foam
down there in the dark, and then below the dark,
in the calm of the still depths (the most tremendous
storm makes no disturbance below nine fathoms).
Will their new world be down on the ocean-floor,
among the caves? Or, following the blown gulls,
through some still gleaming crevice of the sky?
Or will they start again on the green earth,
as newts this time, or leaning-tower giraffes,
or crocodiles who lie still as old tyres
in estuary mud? Or human children
with different facial bones and frizzy hair?
Or will they be the atoms of the water
next time, and hammer some trim ketch to planks
and floating spars? Will they be starfish, lying
five-pointed on the beach these voyagers
would give, in this death-minute, everything
they ever owned to be treading, calmly, now?
Who knows? What we can ask, I think, is
whether death will seem beautiful to them when it comes,
and to us, for that matter, after the pain
is over, I mean. Many great artists have
extolled the beauty of death, have loved and called to it,
and Turner here seems to be saying *now*
I will show you how terror and agony
and the utterly final arrival of death can distil
an essence of beauty – in – terror, an enrichment
in the moment of final relinquishment of all:
as if it took that knowledge, that edge of torment,
to peel away the cataract from our vision, to reveal the beauty of those
mad waters
and that last gleam of light from a hostile day.

Meanwhile, one thing I know: the silent canvas
has stored the howl and thunder of that hour,
the yell of death in the ears of the sacrificed:
the last groan of the timbers, the frantic slap
of the saturated sail. Canvas to canvas. Sound

to silence, through the artist's compassionate mind,
and back to sound again, as I stand here.

Oh, it has 'painterly values' too, and can be discussed
in purely abstract terms: but not now, not now.
Some other time, not in the presence of
the human creatures, air-breathers, gulping their last,
and the sea's roaring that never will be quenched,
and beyond, the starfish at his supine vigil
on the final beach whose shingle we shall be.

Digging for Splinters
(Unpublished poem)

During the green-shoot years
when my sons were growing fast
needing to test their toughness
needing to pit their quickness
against the hard rock's roughness
against the tree-trunk's thickness
they often had me aghast
but I had to suppress my fears.

The grammar of the earth
was what they needed to learn.
Their scampering hard little feet
needed the grain-shift of sand
then with supple toes to meet
the grassy yield inland.
Stone, leaf-mould, moss and fern –
each texture proclaimed its worth.

And of course there were falls from high
and grazes and cuts and bruises.
Untrained but dedicated
I was their microbe-catcher
I slapped on the medicated
plasters, a tireless patcher.
Each roadstead that danger cruises
I seached with my weather-eye.

The job I chiefly dreaded
but felt it my duty to claim
was using a needle to prod
into their skin for jagged
splinters and thorn-tips. God!
Their pain rubbed my own nerves ragged.
I steadied the needle to aim
where the shadow lurked embedded,

and dug and sweated and cursed
as I fretted the skin to lace.
They stood like Indian braves
impassive and watched me wince.
Whimpering was for slaves:
their pride made each one a prince.
A tear-brimmed eye was disgrace –
bella figura came first!

Now they are tall straight men,
their childhood a history-tale;
yet still into living tissue
no longer theirs, but my own
I probe and prod to issue
before they can taint the bone
the dark thorns that assail
and penetrate me now as then.

Still using the same tools
my match to cauterize
the needle's point, my lens
to bring the focus near
my nerves like other men's
shrinking from pain and fear:
I dig for the same prize
though now ambition cools:

Still probing deep for splinters
though no longer splinters of wood
I seek, nor in the skin
that clothes our flesh and bone:
These dark points that push in
lodge in the mind alone,

and to hunt them still fires my blood
though cooled by sixty winters.

Just as, that world ago,
it was not my own pride
that drove me to hunt out
the intruder from their flesh
but love I could not flout
an instinct always fresh
fuelled from deep inside
and lit with a changeless glow.

To bring them out to the light
to hold them in the dramatic
focus we have agreed
to call Art, though truly we
know nothing of Art save the need
to be rid of pain, to be free
of the throbbing and the erratic
pulse in the silence of night.

Held in the light of truth
they show themselves to be
no simple pests, but prizes
worthy of patient pain –
jolts, joys, *trouvailles*, surprises:
as my vision grows sharp again
when my sons replant for me
those hedgerows of their youth.

From Earthtrack, Unpublished Memoirs

Written in the years leading up to 1993 and found among John Wain's papers on his death.

[From the Introduction:]

I have married three times. My first marriage, entered into when I was 22, ended in divorce when I was 30. My second, which lasted from New Year's Day 1960 to my wife's death in June 1988, was to a Welsh lady who was intensely devoted to the language, culture and landscape of Wales. I was already no stranger to North Wales – a glance at the map will show that no one growing up in North Staffordshire could be that – but during the 1960s and 70s I was pulled into a much closer relationship with the country and the people. In terms of the readership for these memoirs, I believe that just as there is an untapped reservoir of Midland readers who will take an interest in the Staffordshire memories of the early part, so the many thoughts and impressions and memories of Wales might easily reach out to a largely untapped Welsh readership. I say 'largely' because I wrote a novel, *A Winter In the Hills* (1970) which I think of as one of the most determined attempts by an English writer to write a novel about Welsh people that will not travesty them as funny little troglodytes but show them as living, breathing people living serious lives. It made its impact, but it has never come into its own, and was in any case 23 years ago. I intend to write freshly of all that rich, tangy subject, tinged with tragedy as the destiny of all minority nations is tinged, outlined for me by a hard black border of finality in that my living passport to inner recesses of Welshhood is gone.

I have said enough about the range of the book, leaving due elbow-room for hares that will start up suddenly during the period of writing – I shan't be afraid to follow them.

For a title, I thought of *Earthtrack*. Thomas Hardy's strange but very characteristic poem, *The Temporary the All'*, contains the line,

Sole the showance these of my onward earth-track,

which when I first read it I found laughable in its quaint diction, but I have never succeeded in forgetting. I would like to write an equally unforgettable book.

JW, 1993

The early summer of 1940 was a particularly brilliant one. As Hitler's armies battered their was across North-West Europe towards their ultimate targer, our island, that island was decked out, increasingly day by day, in her brightest and freshest colours: the varied tints of fresh green in leaf and grass-blade, the cream and pink of blossom, the sparkling of streams running over pebbles. In North Staffordshire as elsewhere, the chestnut trees put out their broad leaves and festive candles, the hawthorn blossom drifted in great suds along the hedges, the cattle from the small farms cropped the meadowgrass in what seemed to the human beholder like a trance of contentment.

As week succeeded week, it became increasingly obvious that Europe was being trodden down under those Nazi boots. All that was something the grown-ups talked about, and even they didn't talk about it all the time or with much confidence that they understood it. 'The War' had still not quite landed on our doorstep, as that doorstep was viewed from North Staffordshire. It was still, until Dunkirk and the Battle of Britain, something that was happening in foreign parts, and foreign parts, at the beginning of 1940, were very foreign indeed. In any case, I was fifteen, which inevitably meant that whatever mgiht be happening on the world stage, my attention was largely taken up by the increase in size of my own body and the development within it of new powers and new needs. I had to adapt to these changes behind a mask of silence and isolation, as most adolescents did in those days. The need for a female companion in bed, which had suddenly appeared in me without much warning and in a full-blown form, was something I had to deal with entirely out of my own resources, which were so limited that they might as well be bluntly described as nil. Within our family circle, I would have been expected to wash my mouth out with soap if I had so much as mentioned the matter. All my friends had the same experience. The attitude our parents uniformly presented to us on these matters, which was simply that they were unmentionable, faced us like an unscaleable fence. The society we came from was inhibited and tongue-tied, governed by very deep taboos, to an extent that anyone born since about 1960 would probably find quite simply incredible.

The problems and conflicts arising from this situation have been thoroughly aired in the English literature of the first half of this century: for instance, in James Joyce's *Portrait of the Artist as a Young Man*. Even the absurd *Lady Chatterley's Lover* has something to teach us here. Otherwise it is a book too poor to be worth mentioning, since the characters are merely cardboard cut-outs behaving as the author has decreed that they must behave in order to demonstrate his thesis (the root cause of the badness of most bad novels). To think *Lady Chatterley's Lover* a masterpiece you must have been subjected to the same kind of sexual repression as I remember, plus some kind of social humiliation that left you with a grudge against the officer-and-gentleman class and a wish to take part vicariously in their humiliation. This latter I escaped, largely I think because my home background, though entirely unpretentious, was very comfortable in a large house and large garden.

All this meant that at the age of fifteen I had more than enough to occupy my attention without having much of an idea of the outside world, and though I am very sure that it was a fault in my family and our *milieu* in general that we were not better informed about international affairs and more intelligent about the probable courseof the war, I think whis was understandable (which is not quite the same thing as pardonable) considering two things. One was that the provinces, in those days, reallly were provincial. In North Staffordshire we had nothing imminent that brought the war physically close. If we had been living in Kent we would have had the Battle of Britain fought out in the sky above our heads. If we had been in Liverpool or Coventry, neither of them very far away, we would have suffered, or at any rate witnessed, appalling air raids. The long ordeal of the Londoners did not begin until 1941, but it must have been obviously in the wings. To us, the war largely meant rumours, shortages and red tape. Plus, of course, the immediate departure of the first wave of young men into the armed services, conscription being introduced only a few months before the war actually started. But, at fifteen, my thoughts were not yet directed ahead to that eventuality.

The other circumstance which helped to explain, without actually excusing, the blissful unawareness of our elders (let alone of us adolescents) was that the powerful and numerous pacifist movement had disseminated a great deal of wish-fulfilment and disinformation. For obvious enough reasons – the most murderous and destructive war in history, after all, was only twenty years behind us – there was an immense grass-roots movement of the never-again persuasion. Many men who had seen trench warfare in the First World War were still only in the early phase of their middle age in 1939, full of vigour (unless indeed they had been incapacitated by the war, which made their testimony more powerful in a different way) and threw themselves passionately into dissuading their countrymen and women from allowing a slide into another conflict, and with the same enemy at that. England, being an island and having a long tradition of political stability and free speech, is not a very politically aware country, and the grasp of most English people on history is still very sketchy; in the inter-war years it was even feebler. The common man had no understanding of the reasons why the 1914 War had broken out or what were the conditions that made Europe a powder-keg in the early years of the century. The war was assumed to have suddenly blown up out of a totally blue sky, which was indeed how most people had experienced it. After 1917, when international socialism became a force in the world and the Communist Party of Great Britain was set up, left-wing opinion vaguely massed itself behind the notion that the war was simply a dirty trick played by silk-hatted millionaires on the working class. (Joan Littlewood evidently went on thinking this well into the 1960s; her immensely successful play, *Oh What A Lovely War*, seemed to be based on the belief that no officers were killled in 1914-18.)

Starting from that basis, it was not very difficult to persuade people that the way to avert a war was simply to declare publicly that you would refuse to take part in it. The general idea was that since politicians were madmen or criminals, the only way to control them was to refuse to follow their instructions if that meant war. A clergyman of the Church of England, H.R.L. Sheppard, initiated a vast movement called the Peace Pledge Union. All you had to do to join it was to write on a post-card the words, 'I renounce war, and will never support or sanction another.' You then sent this postcard to the headquarters of the organization. I don't know how many of these cards they received during the year or so prior to September 3, 1939, but it must have been many hundreds of thousands; millions, I dare say. The participants had an innocent faith that the piling-up of this

Everest of pacific pledges would lead other governments to decide not to attack us, whereas, of course, it acted as a direct invitation to them to do so.

Since the bulk of those who sent in their postcards were obviously decent and gentle people, and probably Sheppard himself was a nice man, it is easy to sympathize with the Peace Pledge Union up to a point, but since its effect was a determined effort to prevent our country from getting ready to repel a savage onslaught, it was plainly a potential disaster, averted only by the fact that the bulk of the populace had too much sense to go along with it. This should have been a lesson so obvious as to be easily learnt, but the fact is that it was not learnt, and exactly the same story was repeated some fifty years later, with CND in the place of the PPU and another deluded clergyman, Bruce Kent, inheriting the role of Sheppard. Once again wiser counsels prevailed, but once again it was only after the situation had been touch and go for some time. Evidently it is a feature of the English mind to throw up structures like the PPU and CND for the same hidden reasons that make lemmings try to solve their problems by rushing down cliffs into the sea. One wonders what form it will take next.

Such, however, was the state of mind of many people at that time, in that flawless early summer of lyrical beauty, before the British Expeditionary Force had been broken and pushed out of France, and before that tiny force of fighter pilots took off from Biggin Hill. John Heath-Stubbs, in his memoirs (*Hindsights*, 1993) recalls how in the immediate pre-war period he was a senior pupil at an English boarding school and was, in time-honoured fashion, sometimes invited by the headmaster, when prominent people came to the school to speak to the boys, to meet them socially at his table. One such visitor was a well-known pacifist, a Quaker with all the authority of that austere sect behind him. In the year of Munich this man assured the company round the table, 'with absolute certainty', that war had come very close during the Munich crisis of a few months previously, and only two things had prevented it: 'One was the united prayers of all Christian people, and the other was that the ordinary Germans had lain themselves down on the railway lines in one of the Berlin stations, thus preventing troop trains from moving forward. This,' Heath-Stubbs goes on, 'was obviously a total fiction and a piece of wishful thinking. It was all too typical of the pacifists at that time.'

This was the intellectual atmosphere that surrounded me; faced with this kind of thing, what option had I but to attend to the things that I could discern clearly, though I had no idea what to do about them? The changes in my body were clear to me; so were my exploding sexual needs, though I had no more chance of having them explode in a manner that would be of any benefit to myself or anyone else than I had of going on a week-end trip to Sirius. That left only two things in my life. One was that my verbal sensibility, which had always been highly developed, had taken giant strides, simply because I had been reading rapidly and hungrily, had been absorbing some French and Latin as part of my routine school work, and was beginning to get the measure of our wonderful English language. Shakespeare made me drunk; I was lifted up to the clouds, as generations of English people before me had been lifted. (Will this work for the generations stretching into the future? Or has it all been too dehydrated, parched, bleached-out, over-systematized, and generally smothered in poisoned droppings from the educational equivalent of laboratory white mice? Have they taken it away from us for ever? If so, I humbly thank God I was born early enough to have my share of it.) The other thing was that my body had become big and strong enough to shove a bicycle along for a good many miles without tiring.The bicycle made me free of the countryside within a wide radius of my home.

And what a countryside! When I see it today, I feel a humble gratitude that it is still undiscovered, so undisturbed by the hyperactive tourist industry. Since I shall never be a best-selling author, I have no fear of attracting the swarm of tour operators, journalists and brochure-writers to my native landscape. I should perhaps explain what I consider my native landscape. Stoke-on-Trent is a long narrow city, a chain of conurbation lying along the valley of the infant river Trent. In my youth it measured ten miles by two. Being too poor to afford any suburbs, it ws a ribbon of mainly industrial buildings, and poor streets. If you faced to either side (it ran pretty exactly from south to north) and walked or cycled for a mile, you got into unspoilt, un-selfconscious countryside. Nowadays, after modest prosperity for so many years, there are suburbs, but nothing daunting. One more detail must be added. This city lies on a hinge. At the southern end it is set among typical Midland dairy-farming country, not very different from the landscape in which Shakespeare grew up. A few miles further on, you cross a geological barrier and enter the North. The Stoke-on-Trent area, with its multiplicity of small steep hills, is in fact the coccyx of the Pennines. If I had been born and bred in Tunstall or Burslem, my native landscape would have had stone walls rather than hedges, the air would have been a degree or two colder, and I would think of myself as a Northerner. But my actual birthplace was Stoke itself, well within the southern sector (they go: Longton, Fenton, Stoke, Hanley, Burslem, and Tunstall) and the nearest countryside was more southern in character. Not only that. When I was three years old, in 1928, my family moved up to the crest of the hill overlooking Stoke, and our view on the non-city side was westward. When I got out my bicycle and pedalled out towards the green spaces, I went through the fringe of Newcasle-under-Lyme (a town much older than the Potteries and sniffy about their enforced proximity). Once I got through that fringe, I was to the west of the Potteries, in an area where Staffordshire almost touches Cheshire and both of them almost touch Shropshire.

The easiest way for anyone to appreciate the landscape which went to the forming of my sensibility, assuming anyone is interested in doing so, is to go to a place called the Dorothy Clive Garden at Willoughbridge, North Staffordshire. It is very easily reached, being on the A5I road midway between Nantwich and Stone. (Since I understand many modern people never go anywhere unless it is on a motorway, I will add that it is reached by Exit 15 from the M6, though I personally would like to dynamite the M6 and every other motorway in England.)

As you emerged into the countryside from Newcastle-under-Lyme, which does have suburbs (I went to school in one of them), your first impression, becoming progressively stronger, is of a series of high ridges. The pottery towns themselves are studded with with abrupt gradients as the Pennines finally run out into a rash of small hills; but once you turn your face to the west and move towards the Shropshire border, the hills give way to long natural folds. As you mount each one you come in sight of a fresh wide sweep of country, and you have a strong sense of liberation from urban chatter, a knwledge that if you go forward and mount the next ridge, and possibly the next one after that, you will be looking at the Welsh marches. The cosy, miniature landscape of the English Midlands, so domesticated, so dear to those who grew up in it, the landscape that stretches from Oxfordshire and

Northamptonshire up to about South Derbyshire, gives way to the higher, more open, more dramatic landscape of wide views and you are climbing up on to the roof of England; over to the west is Wales, with its mountains and valleys and timeless unpopulated stretches of coast. And between you and Wales lie the wide green and blue spaces of Shropshire, where place-names – Ludlow, Clun, Wenlock Edge, Bredon Hill – take the mind back to Housman's poems, those few pages of artfully simple lyric verse that have been unwaveringly present to the English mind, resisting all changes of fashion, effortlessly outselling every new wave, for a hundred years. Housman, boldly staking out a personal claim, called his first collection *A Shropshire Lad*, deliberately importing into his work the suggestion that he was a native of the area he sang about. In fact, the actual historical Alfred Edward Housman was a Worcestershire lad. His birthplace was no nearer to the sacred area of that 'western brookland/ that bred me long ago' than mine was, and though I have never tried to claim any special rights in that magic country I have exactly the same attitude to it as he must have had. Emerging from the Potteries to stand, usually with my bicycle leaning nearby, on the top of one of those long ridges, and gazing westwards in the general direction of market Drayton and Shrewsbury and Oswestry and Llangollen, I felt I had the key to the Shropshire country in my hand, was indeed already treading on its edge.

The Dorothy Clive Garden did not exist in those days. The hill where it now stands was simply open farming country, crowned in this particular case by an abandoned quarry whose sides gave natural shelter to wild saplings and bushes. When Colonel Clive came to design this garden in his wife's memory, he made skilful use of the quarry. Skilful use, indeed, of the entire site. Go there sometime, if you like beautiful places. Mount, on foot or on wheels, to the highest point. Stand and look about. There, stretching mile after mile, is the countryside I first learnt to love. Usung by fame, largely unvisited by sight-seers (thank God), it has a beauty that will at once be acknowledged by everyone. And, since what goes in first goes in deepest, it has remained for more than half a century my fundamental notion of what a beautiful rural landscape should be. Not that I despise other kinds. Not that I have failed to become passionately attached to beautiful landscapes that do not at all resemble this one. But the country between Whitmore and Market Drayton, stretching out towards Woore and Pipe Gate, taking in on the way the hamlet of Black Brook and the more stately manorial village of Maer – blessed names, names loaded with a rural freshness and fragrance and with a beautiful old-fashioned clumsiness about them, like objects made in wood by a patient village craftsman – that country lies at the root of all.

That will do, for the moment, as far as the description of landscape is concerned. I must avoid, even so early in my narrative, giving the impression that I spend a major part of my time and energy gazing about me at my physical surroundings. Still, everyone does spend a fair amount of time doing this, and physical surroundings are important to us all, whether in fully conscious ways or not. To begin with a rough characterization of that Staffordshire-Shropshire-Cheshire area is as good a starting-point as any for an account of what has happened to me in seven decades on Planet Earth. And there are two additional circumstances that help to make the rural environment of my first youth particularly memorable to me. One is that the fateful early summer of 1940 was, as I have said, a particuarly fresh, vivid, fragrant and phhysically delightful time. It would have been so in any case, simply for objective, physical reasons – the weather happened to be glorious. How much more did it seem so as Hitler's armies rushed towards us, armed and prepared for the fatal grapple which would destroy our hastily mustered and under-equipped military forces. At just turned fifteen years old, and deeply rooted in a provincial culture that by tradition took very little notice of what happened abroad, I was still not fully emerged from childhood and tended to leave these matters to the grown-ups; and this, though I think it disgraceful in a great lump of a boy nearly full grown, was an attitude that the same grown-ups had themselves fostered in me; it was very much their own attitude; only a few months earlier, the bulk of the British populace had listened with calm approval while Neville Chamberlain referred to Czechoslovakia as 'a far-away country about which we know little' – or did he actually say 'nothing' – without rising and thundering there and then a demand that the dunderhead be removed from office forthwith and the country placed under responsible leadership.

The other circumstance that makes it tempting and delightful to look back on the May and June of 1940, and to linger there in day-dream, is that it brings back a time lost for ever. Factory farming had not come in. Grazing animals were out in the fields, pigs were in sties, chickens clustered around farmyards. Even horses were no uncommon sight, though already one saw far more of them in central London than in any country district – not that I ever went to central London. The mechanization of agriculture, begun in earnest in about 1917, had continued year by year, but it still had not reached the stage at which a work-force would be necessary. The combine harvester, for example, did not arrive in the English countryside till the mid-forties, after the war had ended. At the time I am speaking of, the average farm had a fair number of workers, though only about one-third as many as it would have had in 1900. Undreamt-of was the state of affairs we have today, when one can travel mile after mile through a rural landscape wihout once seeing a human figure – just endless vistas of land which, while obviously tended, planned for, organized and exploited, has been completely emptied of human beings.

It followed that one of the delights of being in the country, in 1940, was that you met country people there. This had always been so obviously the case that I neither marvelled at it nor had the slightest foreboding that I should one day look back on it with regret and nostalgia. There are evidently no agricultural workers now, in the 1990s. There are, I suppose, though I never see them, a handful of highly trained specialists, urban in their psychology, industrial in their skills, who service the country's agriculture. They don't live in the old tied cottages, but in the nearest towns, driving to to work in the early morning, when the inhabitants of the dormitory villages are getting ready to drive in the opposite direction, heading for town and their offices. In this way, as in just about every other way, the motor car has turned English life inside out.

For this kind of reason, it is all the more important to me, all the more dear to my heart, to look back at a time before this pulling inside out had come to pass. And, since we have gone far enough in these pages without meeting an actual human being and hearing his living voice, it is time for the entry of Mr Nutt.

I met Mr Nutt in that wonderful summer, when he was ninety and I was fifteen. He lived at Black Brook, with his daughter Amy and her huband, Tom Cadman. These good people were small-holders, wringing a living from a patch of ground that would not have supported them without Tom's war pension. A German shell, some time between 1914 and 1918, had cracked open his skull, and in fitting it together they had had to insert a steel plate. It was the availability of countless Tom Cadmans, with their smashed and split bones, that enabled orthopoedic surgery to make such enormous strides during those years. For this and other services to the public weal, Tom received a small weekly pension, on which he and Amy lived in a pretty cottage. I used to visit them there. It was much the same as a similar cottage would have been in the later years of Queen Victoria; it had, for instance, no electricity, being lit perfectly well by brilliant oil lamps which had highly polished metal plates behind the glass shades that contained the wick, to throw out the light by reflection. They were just as good as any lamp you can buy today; you just had to be careful not to knock them over.

Tom and Amy lived in the cottage, while Mr Nutt, who liked his own company, lived in a small wooden shed a few paces from the back door. I was not invited into the shed, nor was anyone else, but I could see from outside that it was about the size to contain a decent-sized bed and perhaps a chair and a dressing-table. But no, Mr Nutt would not have a dressing-table. He would have an ordinary table with a drawer, and probably a wash-stand, with a ewer and a pail. Under the bed would be a chamber-pot. In this domain Mr Nutt, aged ninety, lived when he was not in the cottage having his meals, or out exercising his craft.

The reference to Mr Nutt's craft brings a slight tremor of embarassment to me after more than half a century, because it was the reason why my first conversation with him began with a *gaffe* on my part. Assuming that no man of of fourscore and ten would still be working, I began the dialogue by asking him, 'What did you do, Mr Nutt, before you retired?' He looked at me severely with his bright little button eyes from under the rim of his hard bowler hat and said, 'By goom, I anner retired yet.'

Mr Nutt was, and had been for more than fifty years, a trapper. In our time this word has an ugly ring. It makes one think of spoilt rich women who imagine that their sexual attractiveness will somehow be enhanced if they bedeck their human bodies in the skins of fur-bearing animals who have died an unbelievably cruel death, prolonged over many hours, or at best spent their life in a stinking cage and then been suffocated or electrocuted. The fur trade, as anyone knows who has a shred of sensiblity or intellligence, is simply another, and sickening, atrocity in man's never-ending war on the animals. In Mr Nutt's case, though he would of course have been puzzled by any suggestion that wild animals should be treated with the kindliness one shows to a domestic pet – in his world they were simply a resource – trapping had a different function. Rich women, bank accounts and fashion stores didn't come into it. The country people among who he lived and whose outlook he shared were accustomed to doing without many of the comforts and conveniences of town life. Naturally they made full use of the compensations offered by their rural setting – fresh fish from the lakes and rivers, rabbits and hares for the table, the humbler game birds (pigeons, for instance) in abundance. They were a world apart from the modern townsman who loads up his car with precision weapon and drives out into the countryside at weekends to blaze away at anything that flies or runs or paddles on water. Mr Nutt, in working as a trapper, was partly gathering food (rabbit pie or jugged hare, made by country housewives, helped to put 19th-Century English cooking on a level where it need fear no comparison with French) and partly helping the efforts of farmers, who would call him in to rid a field of some animal that was proving a pest: moles, as a rule, whose skins could then be made into those hard-wearing and comfortable trousers that Victorian workmen wore when they could afford them.

Being self-employed and not on anyone's payroll, Mr Nutt would obviously have no thoughts of retirement as long as he could walk well enough to get round his traps, see well enough to set them accurately, and bend and straighten with enough agility to operate them. He would receive the state Old Age Pension, ten shillings a week (50 pence in our money), and beyond that he would be self-supporting, with the anchorage of his wooden hut and the watchful care of his daughter and son-in-law. This was how it was, and how he would have wanted it to be, as I can appreciate now that I have become something of a Mr Nutt myself.

Working? Of course I'm still working! What else do you expect me to do with my life? And as Mr Nutt, inured to his own company and probably solaced by it, walked along the hedgerows and through the coppices to see if he had gathered anything in his traps, so I take solitary walks through the landscape of my mind to see what ideas, what images, what seeds of narrative, I might find have come to my baits. And sometimes in the actual landscape too, in those places where I can find any hedgerows in it. But there, of course, I touch on one of the great differences between Mr Nutt and myself. After ninety years in the English countryside, Mr Nutt's vision of the future, if he troubled himself to have any vision of the future, would, I am convinced, have been one of steady continuity. When he was gone, someone else would be there, doing the trapping. When the farmers who paid him were gone, other farmers would take their place, living in the same or similar farmhouses. The woods, the lanes, the fields, the wild creatures, would still be there as he remembered them from the days when up in London people were talking about Palmerston and Mr Gladstone, and over in France they was having trouble with them Prooshians. What Mr Nutt could not foresee – and I have no idea how long he lived, for my life took me away from those woods and fields and lanes very soon, leaving them only as a bright indelible memory – was that the rural life he knew was nearing its end, and that the English countryside he probably expected to be eternal would have dwindled, in another thirty-fve years, to a few strips of intensively farmed land to be glimpsed between the motorways, that the villages would have become suburbs, the quiet wayside inns turned into boxes of amplified noise, his whole kingdom not merely dead but buried?

For dead rural England is, and its memorial is that immense wave of country nostalgia that is everywhere in our *Ersatz* culture – in the souvenir shops, in the how-to-live magazines, in the coffee table books, in the educational system which ladles books like *Cider With Rosie* down the throats of children to whom the reality of life is a housing estate. The modern English can't even put up a new glass-and-plastic brewery outlet (I can't call it a 'pub') without calling it 'The Load of Hay' or 'The Dog and Partridge', so deep is the unassuaged longing in them for the land that used to be theirs – theirs to walk about in at least, and to work in, if not (once the Enclosures had taken effect) to enjoy a share in cultivation. Even the strident urban music of the Beatles, spawned in the coffee bars of the late 1950s where the youth culture was incubated, has, if you listen attentively to its melody lines, more than a hint of nostalgia for the tuneful ditties that were minted so easily and naturally in the old country times, the times of Mr Nutt in his youth.

I shall give here no specimen of Mr Nutt's conversation apart from those defiantly uttered six words, 'By goom, I anner retired yet,' because, truth to tell, I do not recall anything else he said. As a man with responsible work in hand, he had no time to squander in talking to a young whippersnapper who began by asking him a foolish question. I could invent conversations in which I gave Mr Nutt some lines to say, and I hope I may claim that they would be, in their way, passably convincing and believable. But if I did so I would be exercising my talent as a novelist, not my skill in the narrower and stricter form of autobiography.

Incidentally, what I think of the modern fashion for writing a bastard mixed form, in which seventy-five percent is a truthful record subject only to the inevitable distortions of memory, and the other twenty-five per cent blatantly invented, will be clear simply from my decisive drawing of the distinction between them. Memory is memory, invention is invention. Just because we are fallible human creatures, the second sometimes creeps in where we intended the first; but to muddle them up deliberately and call the result a new and liberated form of writing is foolishness, arising from complacent vanity. To attempt a symbiosis in which both forms co-exist can only result in tissue rejection and the ruination of both elements.

***

A pot-bank always makes a shawd-ruck. May we have that again, please? A what makes a *what*?

A 'pot-bank', as many people know, is the familiar term in North Staffordshire for a pottery works. Traditionally, and I suppose in some altered form even today, the output of a pot-bank was inspected at regular intervals, (every evening, the way I used to hear it) and divided into Firsts, which were flawless as to firing, finish, glazing, every detail, and Seconds, in which an expert eye could discern, given sufficiently keen attention and a jealous regard for the firm's good name, some tiny fault which left them entirely serviceable but less than formally perfect. These were taken off to be sold, always clearly labelled as Seconds. I have used a fair proportion of them all my life.

The rest, in which even the least judging eye could see faults, were simply carted away to be smashed. They were dumped, in the same unceremonious way that the potters' sister industry, coal-mining, reared its spoils into conical hills that stood about everywhere, towering high above the terraces of dingy little houses. Pit-spoil, with its variegated composition, is inhospitable stuff, but over the generations the heroic perseverance of plants will find a way somehow: tiny roots dig in and cling, tiny green shoots peer up and gather the smokey sunlight, these decay in time into something like a mulch, and somehow a pit-mound (known to the English population at large as a 'slag-heap') becomes covered with patchy green in those areas where it is not daily smothered with a new layer.

Not so a shawd-ruck: we must pause over that word, which signifies a moutain made of broken pottery. I knew it for years before I ever saw it written down, and I have spelt it phonetically. The first syllable, as it actually sounds in North Staffordshire speech, is universally pronounced 'shawd;' roughly, that is, rhyming with 'cord' or 'sword.' This must be simply a pronunciation-variant of 'shard', the usual English word (sometimes spelt 'sherd' but always pronounced 'shard', to rhyme with 'hard') for a piece of broken pottery. When, finally, in middle age I came across the word in print, it was, sure enough, spelt 'shardruck', but the pronunciation is as I have given, and in writing it I instinctively follow the sound I have heard for so many years. I don't mind spelling 'Derby' or 'Berkshire' or 'Cholmondeley' in ways different from the way I speak them, but 'shawd-ruck' is different. 'Shawd-ruck' is mine. It belongs to the old days of the Potteries, like the bottle-kiln with its ring of external fireplaces. Like Stoke City Football Club with their great players, led by the immortal Stanley Matthews, turning out in their trim dark shorts and their shirts with vertical red-and-white stripes, never an advertising slogan between them and never, from one year's end to another, any fights breaking out on the terraces.

A shawdruck, in the old days, was, like so much in the landscape of the Potteries, surreal. It never sprouted even the scantiest layer of vegetation, because it was made entirely of glazed material, rinsed down by every shower of rain, and therefore, without actually being clean (nothing that fell down through our smoke-heavy sky could be called that) kept the glazed surfaces slippery and ungraspable by any form of plant life.

As for the second part of the word, 'ruck', it is obviously a word that in the sturdy, conserving dialect of North Staffordshire, signifies a hill or protuberance of some kind. Even in standard English we say that when something (a pillow, a mattress, a tablecloth) is disarranged and has a ploughed-field surface where it ought to be smooth, it has been 'rucked up.'

***

171

In the autumn of 1947, I went to live in reading, to begin work as a member of the English Department at the University there. That autumn is very clearly engraved on my mind. I was twenty-two and my wife twenty-three; we had been married a few weeks. Our marriage was not going well; it never did go well; but that was nobody's fault in particular. It was on a loser from the beginning,and I think we knew it. I remember that autumn as a time of high gusty winds and thick drifts of rich fallen leaves, still dramatic in colouring although they were dead. As a first step to 'finding somewhere to live', we had taken furnished rooms in Caversham, which in those days (I don't know what it is like now) was a dignified suburb across the river from the town of Reading and therefore in Berkshire. The left bank of the Thames, at that point and for some miles before it, is high and steeply sloping, so that as soon as you crossed Caversham Bridge and began to move into Caversham itself you began climbing, toiling upwards with large, stately houses on either side, their gardens full of established trees that made the area as leafy as North Oxford, which must have been partly why we found it attractive.

The house where we had rented some space was in a short, select and quiet thoroughfare named Derby Road. It was Victorian, or at the very least Edwardian – but no, surely only Victoria could have presided over an England confident enough to house her business and professional classes in such quiet, opulent dignity, amid such well-planned, well-tended greenhouses and stables. It was like a slighter, smaller but even more self-possessed, version of the house in Dresden [an area of Stoke-on-Trent where the writer first went to infant school] where my kindergarten had dragged out its bumpy existence. We had a sitting room on the ground floor and a tiny bedroom at the top of the house, just under the roof. We cooked our food in the shared kitchen and carried it into the sitting-room to eat it. Our immediate landlady was a woman in her thirties with a small daughter whose husband, we were told, was an RAF officer who had chosen to make the Air Force his career and would therefore not be demobilized; the couple were, like almost everyone in post-war England, 'looking for a house', though as he never appeared I sometimes speculated that they might have split up.

Such, setting aside my daily hours at the University, where I began my teaching career by taking a weekly class on Chaucer – was the setting of my outer life. My inner life concerned itself entirely with poetry. I thought poetry, dreamed poetry, ate and drank and read and considered and discussed poetry. As naturally as all these, I also wrote poetry. Mostly I was dissatisfied with the result, a healthy enough state to be in, at the age of twenty-two. I had yet, at that stage, to settle on a manner or a diction that seemd to me to contain naturally the kind of things I wanted to say. Since I was always reading one poet or another, it followed that the space thus left empty in my poetic mind was always being occupied by a presiding genius. Many of these did not last long, but at least an equal number passed into the deeper layers of my mind and entered the pantheon of my 'favourite poets', who now, as I look back on the threshold of old age, number about a ten or a dozen. Most of these were passionately devoured and assimilated during those first months at Reading. No wonder Reading is an important place to me. A place of the mind, I should add, since it has changed virtually beyond recognition (even the University is not where it was when I used to work there), and I have never been back to Caversham since about 1950, for fear of what I should find. But the poets kept up their stately progression though my head. One after another, they took possession of my mind. In the summer before I went to live in Caversham, it was the work of Dylan Thomas that obsessed me. But in those first few Caversham weeks, in that blowy, leafy autumn, it was the time of Wilfred Owen.

I did not, in those days, approach poetry through biography. It was quite usual for me to become very familiar with a poet's work, to spend years, intermittently, concentrating on it and distilling out its essences, with only the sketchiest knowledge of the life of the individual behind it. After all, why should *that* be interesting? I knew that my own life wasn't interesting, yet I hoped that my mind, and one day soon my work, might reveal itself as powerful and original. In the case of Wilfred Owen, I became fascinated simply on the strength of a few poems of his I read in an anthology. (Most people who love poetry will admit readily that anthologies have been important to them in suggesting guide-lines and directions, which is why anthologies are important. I have always believed in them and have edited at least half a dozen myself.)

Owen's poetry made an immediate conquest of me. I knew of him only as a young poet of some thirty years ago, who had been killed towards the end of the First World War when he was about the age that I was at the time I began reading him. I used to murmur his poems to myself – for of course I immediately got large chunks of them by heart, simply by reading them so many times – as I walked about, if I happened to be alone. ....

The manuscript ends here.

SELECT BIBLIOGRAPHY

Novels:

Hurry On Down, 1953
Living in the Present, 1955
The Contenders, 1958 (dramatised on ITV)
A Travelling Woman, 1959
Strike the Father Dead, 1962
The Young Visitors, 1965
The Smaller Sky, 1967
A Winter In the Hills, 1970
The Pardoner's Tale, 1978
Lizzie's Floating Shop, 1981 (teenage fiction)
Young Shoulders, 1982 (dramatised for BBC TV)
The Oxford Trilogy:
    Where the Rivers Meet, 1988
    Comedies, 1991
    Hungry Generations, 1994

Poetry:

Mixed Feelings, 1951
A Word Carved on a Sill, 1956
Weep Before God, 1961
Wildtrack, 1965
Letters to Five Artists, 1969
Feng, 1975
Poems 1949-79
Poems for the Zodiac, 1980
The Seafarer (trans.), 1980
Open Country, 1986

Criticism and Essays:

Preliminary Essays 1957
The Living World of Shakespeare, 1964
A House for the Truth,1972
Professing Poetry,1977

Biography:

Samuel Johnson, 1974

Autobiography:

Sprightly Running 1962
Dear Shadows, portraits from memory, 1986

Drama:

Harry in the Night, 1975 (stage)
Johnson is Leaving 1994 (stage)
Frank, 1982 (radio)
Hypatia, 1992 (radio)

Short Story Collections:

Nuncle and Other Stories 1960
Death of the Hind Legs,1966
The Lifeguard, 1971

Edited:

Interpretations,1955
Anthology of Modern Poetry, 1963
Selected Poems of Thomas Hardy, 1966
Johnson As Critic,1973
Johnson on Johnson,1976
Everyman's Book of English Verse, 1981
The Oxford Library of English Poetry,1986
The Oxford Library of Short Novels,1990
The Journals of James Boswell, 1991

Travel articles :

Various, including articles on Normandy and Brittany
in the Insight Guide to France:

Collections and Manuscripts

There are four major John Wain collections. The Bodleian Library in
Oxford houses a special collection of his original first editions,
including translations. There are collections of all his major published
works at the Library, University of Reading, and at the Central
Library in Hanley, Stoke-on-Trent.

There are a large number of John Wain's original manuscripts
housed at Edinburgh University Library, George Square, Edinburgh.
This last also has a much literary and personal correspondence to
Wain, including letters from Philip Larkin – the full collection of
letters gives a picture of a rather warmer relationship between the two
than the published selection manages.

Further Reading

The Inkings, Humphrey Carpenter, 1978
Account of C.S. Lewis, Tolkien, Charles Williams and their circle at
Oxford, including details of John Wain's contact with and opinion of
the circle.

John Wain: Man of Letters, Elizabeth Hatziolou, 1997, Pisces Press.
Full length critical and biographical study of John Wain.
Available from Pisces Press, contact Smaller Sky Books.

John Wain, by Dale Salwak, Boston, Twayne, 1981
Book length critical study.

John Wain – A Bibliography, David Gerard, Mansell Publishing Ltd
1987

*By arrangement with the Estate of John Wain, Smaller Sky Books has a
limited number of copies of the following books available in their original
bindings.*

Johnson is Leaving – *a play by John Wain, published by Pisces Press
1994. John Wain's last work, a moving study of the last days of Dr Johnson.*

The Lifeguard. *Stories by John Wain from 1975.*

Wildtrack.*Book length poem from 1965.*

Professing Poetry, 1977

The first two novels in the Oxford Trilogy:

Where the Rivers Meet, paperback.

Comedies, paperback.

ed. **The Collected Journals of James Boswell,** in hardback or paperback.

Young Shoulders, *the winner of the Whitbread Literary Award 1984, subsequently made into a BBC TV drama. Hardback.*

Please contact Smaller Sky to order or enquire about these titles.

OTHER TITLES FROM SMALLER SKY

Dictators by Brian Glanville, acclaimed novelist and one of Britain's best football writers.

Two charismatic figures face each other on the world stage: Arturo Toscanini, the great Italian conductor, and Benito Mussolini, leader of Fascist Italy. As the two attack each other in words, the great maestro is threatened by the dictator's thugs – but he will not back down, no matter what the cost to his loved ones. And as Europe explodes into warfare, it is a young New York journalist who follows the strange feud between the pair to its final dangerous conclusion.

'How rare a thing, a novelist who knows his Italy'
Daily Telegraph

Paperback, £8.99   ISBN 1903100038

Scenes From Death and Life by William Cooper.

William Cooper has been called the godfather of the Angry Young Men. This, his final novel, published in 1999, tells the latest episode in the story of Joe Lunn, his semi-autobiographical hero. It is a story of love and loss, shot through with Cooper's own particular brand of dry wit and gentle observation.

'Highly recommended…is anyone ever going to recognise William Cooper's contribution to the modern novel?
Private Eye

'..a triumph…astonishing shifts of gear and emotional temperature…'
The Independent

'As wise, true and witty as any he has written…imagination playing on experience and memory'
Daily Telegraph

Paperback £7.99   ISBN 1903100003

Not Too Late For Loving *– A Lifetime of Occasional Verse*
by Graham Tayar.

Graham Tayar writes:

'I've written on love, marriage (several in fact!), politics, loss, death, on and for my children and grandchildren, and about anything that struck me at the time as funny, odd, poignant or inexplicable. God and the English language fall into this category.'

'Poems both charming and evocative; a collection to enjoy and make you think hard.'
> *Alice Thomas Ellis*

Paperback, £8.99   ISBN 190310002X

To order these titles, visit your local bookshop, order through Amazon.com or write to Smaller Sky Books or email us at order@smallersky.com

www.smallersky.com has a website set up to promote new writing talent as well as established authors. We have extracts from new novels and poetry free on the site, or you can order a printed copy or a text file of new novels, literature and thrillers.

We welcome **new authors** – please contact us via the site or by writing to Smaller Sky Books, 10 Brook Hill, Woodstock, Oxford, OX20 1XH – no unsolicited manuscripts please.